D1507486

SKILL SHARPENERS
Geography
4

Writing: Mike Graf
Editing: Lisa Vitarisi Mathews
Copy Editing: Cathy Harber
Art Direction: Yuki Meyer
Design/Production: Yuki Meyer
Jessica Onken

EMC 3744

Evan-Moor®
Helping Children Learn

Visit
teaching-standards.com
to view a correlation
of this book.
This is a free service.

**Correlated to
Current Standards**

EVAN-MOOR CORP.
phone 1-800-777-4362, fax 1-800-777-4332.
Entire contents © 2018 EVAN-MOOR CORP.
18 Lower Ragsdale Drive, Monterey, CA 93940-5746. Printed in China

CPSIA: Asia Pacific Offset Ltd, Kowloon, Hong Kong [01/2021]

Contents

Essential Element: Human Systems

Contents, continued

Around the World

Concept:
A globe is a geographic representation of Earth.

Last year I received a globe for my 10th birthday. I took it into my room and studied it as I thought about the people in my family. First, I tilted it so I could look at South America. I have cousins who live in Peru and Ecuador. I noticed that they live very close to the equator.

Next, I spun the globe to Africa, noticing all the countries there. I remembered the trip my parents took to Kenya and Tanzania a few years ago. Once a year, they take out the wildlife pictures they took and we all look at them. I hoped one day I could go on a safari there as well.

I traced the globe north across the equator into Asia where I located India. My uncle is from India. I found his home city of Delhi. Next, I went north again to Tibet and China. I saw the long chain of the Himalaya Mountains along the way. I figured I was getting pretty close to Mount Everest, but I was anxious to spin the globe. So I moved on before I found it.

Before spinning the globe toward home in North America, I stopped to inspect New Zealand and Australia. Once again, I was south of the equator. After I finished my imaginary travels, I realized I had gone around the world. I hoped one day I would be able to do it for real!

The World in Spatial Terms

Earth's Seasons

The World in Spatial Terms

Most globes have lines that run from left to right and top to bottom. The main line right in the middle of the globe is the equator. The lines that are parallel to, or stay equal distance below and above, the equator are called latitude lines.

These lines help show many things. One is where seasons occur. The center of the Earth, or the area around the equator, gets the most direct sunlight year-round. But the farther north or south you move from the equator, the amount of sunlight changes because of Earth's tilt. The resulting amount of sunlight creates the seasons.

A city like Singapore, which is only 1 degree north of the equator, has warm temperatures all year long. The latitude of Washington, DC, is 39 degrees north. The winters there are cold but the summers are very warm. The temperatures vary even more in Moscow, Russia, which is 56 degrees north of the equator. Moscow has very cold winters, and its summer afternoons are cool, too. So, the farther away from the equator a place is located, the cooler the weather gets overall and the more it changes with each season.

Define It!

equator: the very center line on the globe

parallel: always an equal distance apart

seasons: when weather changes from one time of year to another

Answer the items.

1. Would you want to live close to the equator, or north or south of the equator? Explain why.

   _____

   _____

2. Why do people near the equator have fewer seasonal changes?

   _____

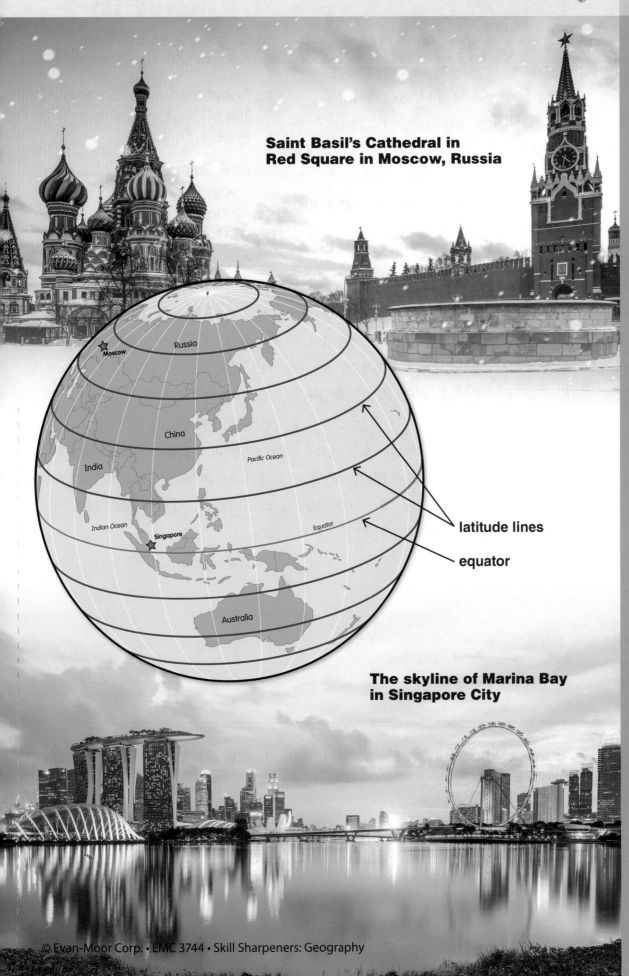

Saint Basil's Cathedral in Red Square in Moscow, Russia

latitude lines

equator

The skyline of Marina Bay in Singapore City

The World in Spatial Terms

Concept:
A globe is a geographic representation of Earth.

The World in Spatial Terms

East and West

A globe has lines that go north to south. These are called lines of longitude. One of these lines is called the prime meridian. It goes directly through Greenwich, England. This line is at 0 degrees longitude.

Other longitude lines are shown in degrees east or west of the prime meridian. For example, the city of Auckland, New Zealand, is 174 degrees east longitude. Tokyo, Japan, is 139 degrees east. Beijing, China, is 116 degrees east. Lima, Peru, is 77 degrees west. Mexico City, Mexico, is 99 degrees west. And New York City, New York, in the United States is 74 degrees west longitude.

Knowing longitude and latitude is important for many things, including ocean navigation. Navigation is controlling the movement of a boat or ship from one place to another. Instruments can tell us our ocean location. They can also guide us to desired destinations by using latitude and longitude coordinates.

Answer the items.

1. What is the prime meridian?

   _____

   _____

2. Can you find your city's nearest longitude line on a globe? What is it, including *east* or *west*?

   _____

   _____

Skill Sharpeners: Geography • EMC 3744 • © Evan-Moor Corp.

The Kwame Nkrumah Memorial
Park is in Accra, Ghana.

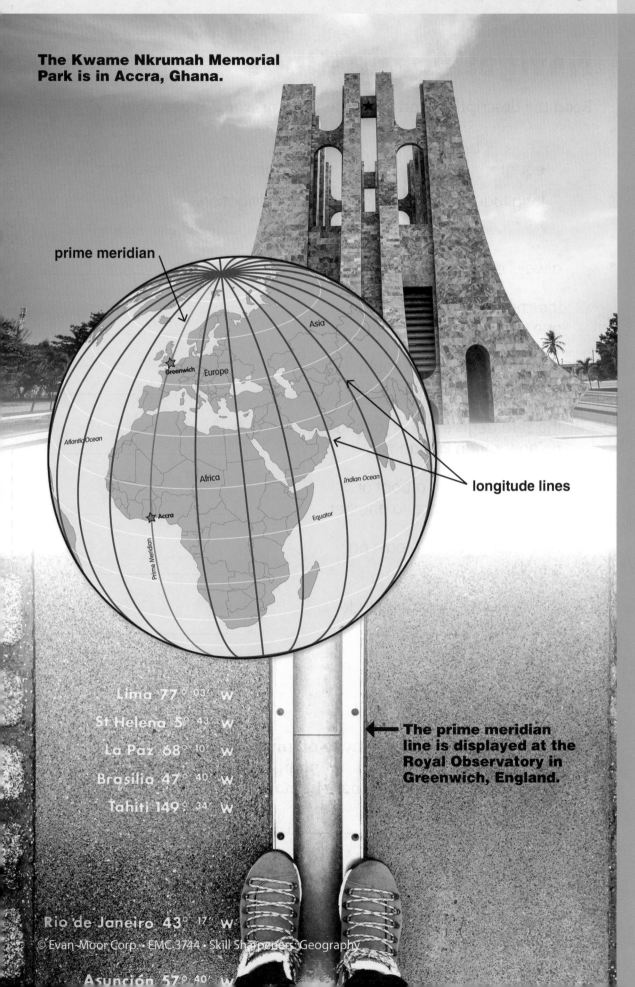

prime meridian

Asia

Greenwich Europe

Atlantic Ocean

Africa

Indian Ocean

Accra

Prime Meridian

Equator

longitude lines

Lima 77° 03' W

St Helena 5° 43' W

La Paz 68° 10' W

Brasilia 47° 40' W

Tahiti 149° 34' W

← The prime meridian
line is displayed at the
Royal Observatory in
Greenwich, England.

Rio de Janeiro 43° 17' W

Asunción 57° 40' W

The World in Spatial Terms

Skill:
Apply content vocabulary in context

Navigating the Globe

Read the description and write the word or words it describes.

equator	parallel	latitude	seasons
longitude	prime meridian	navigation	

1. always equal distance apart _____

2. the change of weather from one time of year to another _____

3. lines that go north to south on a globe _____

4. the zero degree line of longitude going through England _____

5. the act of guiding a boat or ship from one place to another _____

6. lines that go west to east on a globe _____

7. the very center line of latitude on a globe _____

Think About It

Can you think of any other way to organize the globe on a grid system? Does your new way of setting up navigation make things easier to find places or more challenging?

_____

_____

The World in Spatial Terms

Skill Sharpeners: Geography • EMC 3744 • © Evan-Moor Corp.

Finding Places on the Globe

In this activity, you will teach yourself and others how to find places on the globe by using latitude and longitude lines.

What You Need

- globe or world map
- paper
- pencil
- tape or small sticky notes

What You Do

1. Use tape or small sticky notes to mark five locations where latitude and longitude lines intersect on a globe or world map.

2. Write the name of the location or landmark and its latitude and longitude degrees and directions. For example: Graz, Austria, latitude 47° north, longitude 15° east.

3. Explain latitude and longitude to friends or family members.

4. Then tell them the exact latitude and longitude and degrees and directions of one of your landmarks. Ask if they can find it on the globe or map. Repeat with the other four locations you chose.

5. After all five locations have been identified, switch roles and have someone choose five places for you to find based on their latitude and longitude and directions.

The World in Spatial Terms

Taking Away the Lines

Skill:
Write explanatory text to convey information clearly

What if there were no such thing as latitude or longitude lines for navigation? How would you describe to someone where something is located on a globe? Try to do it. Describe to someone where something is located on a globe without using latitude and longitude. Write about the challenges you faced and tell if you were able to overcome them.

_____

_____

_____

_____

_____

_____

_____

_____

_____

_____

_____

_____

_____

The World in Spatial Terms

The Bermuda Triangle

Concept:
As exploration expanded around the globe, perceptions of the world changed.

My parents and I were on a long cruise. We traveled from Florida and out into the Caribbean. We landed at several ports, including Puerto Rico. It had been a great vacation so far. Now we were somewhere in the Atlantic Ocean. I stood there with my mom and dad and looked out over the vast sea. We couldn't

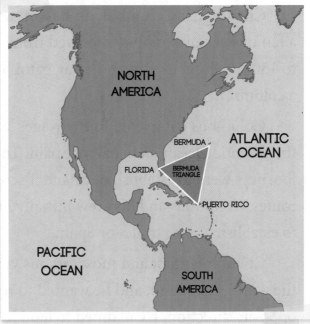

see land in any direction. Then my dad spoke quietly, "I think we are in the Bermuda Triangle now," he said with a hint of fear in his voice.

Mom chimed in nervously, "Do you have to bring that up now?"

Dad replied, "Oh, I'm not serious. All those disappearances were just rumors and exaggerations."

I then asked, "What's this all about?"

Dad explained, "This part of the Atlantic is called the Bermuda Triangle. It has been rumored for a long time to cause ships and planes to disappear. There are many explanations for this, including erratic and violent weather. But none of them have ever been proven true."

Still, for a short time the three of us stood looking out at the ocean. I have to admit that for a moment, I wondered how Columbus and other early explorers made it through this area. I also wondered how many ancient ships lie in the waters below us, never to be heard from again. Would we ever return to land again?

We did. Three days later, we arrived back in Florida safe and sound.

The World in Spatial Terms

Columbus

The World in Spatial Terms

Christopher Columbus, an Italian, was a famous ocean explorer who lived from 1451 to 1506. Columbus was also a navigator and a colonizer.

Columbus completed four voyages across the Atlantic Ocean on behalf of Spain. The journeys were to establish permanent settlements and to set up trade routes. Columbus and his crew initially intended to reach the East Indies to establish a spice trade for Spain.

Columbus's first and most famous voyage was in 1492. He knew the world was round, and he wanted to reach the Far East by going an opposite direction. He planned to land in Japan but instead reached the "New World." Columbus ported in the Bahamas, which he called San Salvador. Three more voyages led Columbus to set foot in the Caribbean, Venezuela, and Central America. These expeditions established the first regular contact between Europeans and the Americas. Columbus called the people he encountered on the new lands Indios, which is Spanish for "Indians." After Columbus, other explorers continued to make ocean expeditions for hundreds of years.

Define It!

colonizer: someone who settles new lands for a country

trade: exchanging one product for another

Indios: Columbus's word for "Indians"

Answer the items.

1. Why were Columbus's voyages important?

   _____

   _____

2. Why do you think Columbus was chosen to head the voyages?

   _____

   _____

*The Landing of Columbus,
October 11, 1492 – Painting
by Currier & Ives, 1846*

The World in Spatial Terms

Magellan

The World in Spatial Terms

Define It!

fleet: a group of ships sailing together

strait: a narrow passage of water connecting two larger areas

circumnavigation: traveling completely around something

Ferdinand Magellan was a famous Portuguese explorer during the 16th century. As a child, Magellan studied map-making and navigation. He later became an expert sailor. King Charles of Spain chose him to sail on a journey searching for a new westward route to the Maluku Islands, also called the Spice Islands.

In 1519, Magellan took command of a five-vessel fleet and 270 men. He sailed across the stormy Atlantic and faced many hardships. During the voyage, one ship wrecked and another ship with its crew deserted, or left, the journey. People were worried that the expedition was doomed. Then Magellan and three of his ships got stuck in what is now called the Strait of Magellan, but after 38 days, they eventually made it through. In 1521, Magellan was killed in a battle on the way to the Spice Islands. Juan Sebastián Elcano took command after Magellan's death and successfully led two ships to the Spice Islands.

In the end, Magellan's journey became what is now known as the first circumnavigation—meaning they sailed around the world! Unfortunately, Magellan did not complete the entire journey. But after three years, one ship and 18 of the remaining crew members made it all the way around the world, returning to Spain in 1522.

Answer the item.

Why do you think the people on the ships thought the voyage was doomed?

_____

_____

_____

Skill Sharpeners: Geography • EMC 3744 • © Evan-Moor Corp.

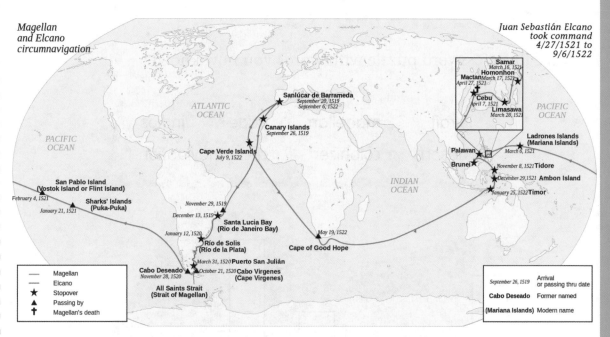

Magellan and Elcano circumnavigation

Juan Sebastián Elcano took command 4/27/1521 to 9/6/1522

ATLANTIC OCEAN

PACIFIC OCEAN

PACIFIC OCEAN

INDIAN OCEAN

Sanlúcar de Barrameda
September 20, 1519
September 6, 1522

Canary Islands
September 26, 1519

Cape Verde Islands
July 9, 1522

San Pablo Island
(Vostok Island or Flint Island)
February 4, 1521

Sharks' Islands
(Puka-Puka)
January 21, 1521

November 29, 1519

December 13, 1519

Santa Lucia Bay
(Rio de Janeiro Bay)

January 12, 1520

Río de Solis
(Río de la Plata)

May 19, 1522

Cape of Good Hope

March 31, 1520 Puerto San Julián

Cabo Deseado   *October 21, 1520* Cabo Virgenes
November 28, 1520   (Cape Virgenes)

All Saints Strait
(Strait of Magellan)

Samar
March 16, 1521
Homonhon
Mactan *March 17, 1521*
April 27, 1521
Cebu
April 7, 1521
Limasawa
March 28, 1521

Ladrones Islands
(Mariana Islands)

Palawan   *March 6, 1521*

Brunei

November 8, 1521 Tidore

December 29, 1521 Ambon Island

January 25, 1522 Timor

— Magellan
— Elcano
★ Stopover
▲ Passing by
✝ Magellan's death

September 26, 1519 — Arrival or passing thru date
Cabo Deseado — Former named
(Mariana Islands) — Modern name

French map of the first world circumnavigation of Ferdinand Magellan and Juan Sebastián Elcano, from 1519 to 1522

Replica of Magellan's ship, *Nao Victoria,* in Punta Arenas, Chile

The World in Spatial Terms

Around the World

Solve this crossword puzzle with words you now know!

strait   magellan   trade   indios

desert   colonizer   circumnavigation

The World in Spatial Terms

Down

1. someone who settles land for a country
2. to leave something or someone behind
3. narrow passage of water
4. exchanging one item for another
6. Portuguese explorer
7. Columbus's name for Indians

Across

5. to go completely around something

Skill Sharpeners: Geography • EMC 3744 • © Evan-Moor Corp.

Care Package

In this activity, you will put together a care package for one of the explorers in this unit.

Skill:
Apply geography concepts in real-world situations

What You Need

- shoe box
- 10 items to include in a care package

What You Do

1. Pretend you know Columbus or Magellan or someone in their crew. You also know he will be at sea for a long time, maybe for several years. Think about things he may need and things he might like to have.

2. Write the items you'd like to include in the care package. The items should be important, special, and able to last the long voyage.

3. Place the items in the shoe box.

4. Pretend someone in your family is the person you chose. Give him or her the box.

Items in Care Package

_____   _____

_____   _____

_____   _____

_____   _____

_____   _____

The World in Spatial Terms

Ocean Voyage Journal

Skill:
Write narrative text about real-world situations

Pretend that you have been at sea for months and months and you finally see land. Write a journal entry about what life has been like on the ship and what you want to do once you reach land.

The World in Spatial Terms

National Park Summer

Yosemite

Grand Canyon

Last summer my family and I decided to visit national parks in the United States. Along the way, we saw some of the world's best places. Our expedition began at Yosemite National Park in California. We saw glorious waterfalls and huge cliffs. Next, we made the trek to Arizona to see the mile-deep Grand Canyon. From there we drove to several national parks in Utah, including Zion, Bryce Canyon, and Arches. My favorite park in Utah was Arches. I was in awe as I looked at Delicate Arch, standing all by itself. Next, we headed north to Glacier National Park in Montana. Seeing the view from Going-to-the-Sun Road was jaw-dropping. Then we went south to visit the world's first national park created in 1872, Yellowstone National Park. Old Faithful Geyser did *not* disappoint! Then we journeyed west to Olympic National Park in Washington. We explored the wettest place on the continent and the rainforest there. Finally, we headed home for one more stop, Crater Lake National Park in Oregon. Boy, was that lake ever deep blue! This was the best summer of my life!

Arches

Olympic

Crater Lake

Places and Regions

Concept:
Places are locations that have distinctive physical and human characteristics.

New Zealand

Define It!

hemisphere: one half of the Earth

glacier: large sheets of ice that move slowly

fiord: a U-shaped glacier-carved valley that was once flooded by the sea

National parks are special lands that countries preserve and protect. New Zealand, in the Southern Hemisphere, has 13 national parks.

New Zealand is made up of two islands—the North Island and the South Island, which are both long and thin. Starting on the North Island, a popular national park is Tongariro. This national park is New Zealand's oldest, and it has glaciers as well as three active volcanoes.

Most of New Zealand's most famous national parks are on the South Island. Abel Tasman National Park is one known for its incredible beaches. Aoraki/Mount Cook National Park has massive glaciers hanging off its sides. The huge glaciers move slowly downhill. Westland National Park has rainforests and two very large glaciers, the Franz Josef and the Fox.

The country's most famous and its largest national park is Fiordland. It has 14 large fiords that are framed by high mountains, waterfalls, and many lakes and rivers. In 1990, Fiordland was listed as a United Nations World Heritage Site and given the name Te Wahipounamu, meaning "the place of greenstone," after the area's most treasured mineral resource, jade. Fiordland is also where a number of scenes from the movie *Lord of the Rings* were filmed.

Answer the items.

1. Would you like to visit New Zealand's North Island or South Island? Explain your answer.

_____

_____

2. In your opinion, what is the most special thing about Fiordland?

_____

Emerald Lakes in Tongariro National Park, North Island, New Zealand

Mt. Cook viewed from Mt. Fox – Fox Glacier in Westland National Park, South Island, New Zealand

Milford Sound in Fiordland National Park, South Island, New Zealand

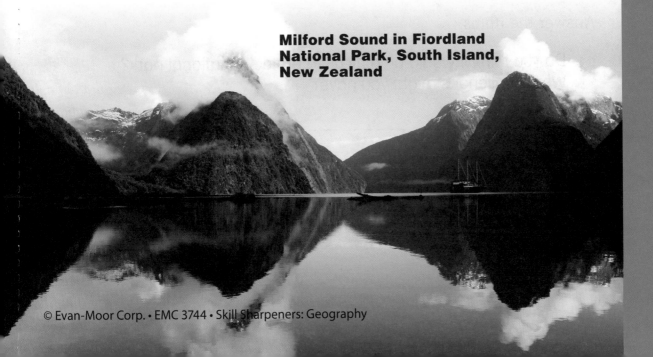

Places and Regions

Down Under

Concept:
Places are locations that have distinctive physical and human characteristics.

The country of Australia, also in the Southern Hemisphere, has 516 national parks—the most in the world. These special places were preserved for their natural beauty. The national parks also protect all the flora and fauna found there.

One famous national park in Australia is Purnululu. This park has colorful beehive-shaped hills that are extremely photogenic. This park also has preserved Aboriginal rock art that is thousands of years old.

Uluru-Kata Tjuta National Park is in the very center of Australia. It is most famous for Uluru (massive Ayers Rock) and the Kata Tjuta (the Olgas, a grand range of red domed mountains). The national park also has sacred Aboriginal sites.

Finally, Kakadu National Park in Northern Australia is the country's largest national park. Native Aboriginals have lived at Kakadu for up to 40,000 years. Kakadu has many rare or endangered plants and animals protected there. In fact, more than 280 different types of birds and 2,000 plants flourish at Kakadu.

Define It!

flora: natural plants of a region

fauna: natural animals of a region

endangered: a very rare plant or animal

Answer the items.

1. Do you think it would be difficult to protect a national park? What challenges might you have?

_____

_____

2. Why do you think Australia has so many national parks?

_____

Places and Regions

Majestic Uluru at sunrise in the Northern Territory, Australia

Comb-crested jacana on the Yellow River in Kakadu National Park, Northern Territory

Aboriginal tour guide demonstrating a Woomera spearthrower at Kakadu National Park, Northern Territory

Bungle Bungles in Purnululu National Park, Western Australia

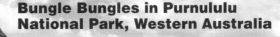

Places and Regions

Skill:

Apply content vocabulary in context

Special Places

Read the description and write the word or words it describes.

| flora | fauna | national park | hemisphere |
| glacier | fiord | endangered | |

1. the animals of a region _____

2. a special area of land protected by a country _____

3. an ice sheet that slowly melts and moves downhill _____

4. the plants of a region _____

5. one of two halves of the Earth, divided at the center _____

6. an inland body of water that is deep and narrow and connected to the sea _____

7. a very rare plant or animal _____

Think About It

What are some reasons a certain area might be made into a national park? Why would a country want to protect certain lands?

_____

_____

_____

_____

Places and Regions

Skill Sharpeners: Geography • EMC 3744 • © Evan-Moor Corp.

National Park Trivia

Make national park trivia
cards and play a game with
your family.

What You Need

- index cards
- Internet access

What You Do

1. Research the most famous
national parks around the
world. Come up with details,
clues, and questions to write
on index cards about each
park or famous sites at the
parks. Example: Old Faithful
Geyser in Yellowstone.
(You may wish to include
the examples shown.

2. Ask your family to play the
trivia game with you. One
player reads a card, and the
other players try to guess
which national park or famous
site is being described.

Old Faithful Geyser can be found
in which national park?

answer: Yellowstone

Which national park could be called
"the grandest" of all?

answer: The Grand Canyon

In which New Zealand national
park are large Ice Age forms found?

answer: Aoraki/Mount Cook
National Park

Places and Regions

Skill:
Write persuasive text

A Future National Park

Think of a special place near you that should be made into a national park. Write a letter to the International Union for Conservation of Nature (IUCN), asking them to make the site you choose a national park. Include details that will persuade the group to agree with you.

Dear IUCN,

_____

_____

_____

_____

_____

_____

_____

_____

_____

_____

_____

Places and Regions

Skill Sharpeners: Geography • EMC 3744 • © Evan-Moor Corp.

Stuck in the Ice

Concept:
Places are locations that have distinctive physical and human characteristics.

My grandfather is a sailor. One day we took his boat out for a journey around Martha's Vineyard in Massachusetts. That day, Grandpa told me a story I will never forget. It was about a man named Shackleton. He and his crew had an unforgettable boating expedition between 1914 and 1917. They wanted to cross the continent of Antarctica.

Here is what Grandpa said…"They left in their spring, which is our fall. They planned to get through ice near the South Pole as it melted. But the ice that year was incredibly thick. Their boat, the *Endurance,* got stuck and drifted in the ice for many months. Eventually, as their summer passed into winter, the ice built up so much that it broke the ship. They had to remove their supplies and camp, and they used lifeboats from there on. But the journey was far from over."

"Stop, Grandpa!" I complained. "Do you want me to be a sailor or not when I grow up?"

Grandpa smiled. "You're right. I don't want to scare you away from the ocean." Then he said, "Do me a favor and read about Shackleton's voyage when you are ready, okay?"

I agreed.

But Grandpa snuck in one more bit of information. "Somehow or another, Shackleton made it back safely."

Places and Regions

Antarctica

Places and Regions

Define It!

South Pole: the southernmost place on Earth

breed: to have babies

continent: one of Earth's seven large landmasses

Earth's southernmost continent is Antarctica. The South Pole is located on Antarctica.

The continent, which is one of Earth's seven large landmasses, was first discovered in 1820 by a Russian expedition. Until then, no one is known to have lived there. Antarctica owns the world record for lowest temperature, 129°F (54°C). Most of the world's ice is there. Antarctica is colder than the Arctic, where the North Pole is, for several reasons. One is that it is higher in elevation due to the thick ice and mountains. Some of Antarctica's ice is several miles thick! Also, the seas around it are colder than the Arctic Sea. And there is less direct sunlight on Antarctica than on any land on Earth. Winters from late March until September are entirely dark.

There are very few plants on Antarctica because it is so cold. Whales, orcas, seals, and colossal squids live in the waters around Antarctica. Antarctica's most famous animal is the penguin. Several types breed on land there, including the world's largest penguin, the emperor penguin. There are no towns on Antarctica, but several countries have their research stations there.

Answer the items.

1. Why do you think few people visit Antarctica?

   _____

   _____

2. Why do you think it took so long for the continent to be discovered?

   _____

   _____

Skill Sharpeners: Geography • EMC 3744 • © Evan-Moor Corp.

Emperor penguin colony near an iceberg in Antarctica

Killer whales in Antarctica's frigid waters

The Arctic

Concept:

Places are locations that have distinctive physical and human characteristics.

Places and Regions

The northernmost part of the Earth is called the Arctic Circle. This area is mostly ocean. Parts of several countries are within the Arctic Circle, including Alaska (in the United States), Canada, Finland, Greenland, Iceland, Norway, Russia, and Sweden. The Arctic Ocean is mostly full of ice. In recent years that ice has been melting due to climate change. The land around the Arctic Circle is without trees. It has permafrost, which means there is a thick layer of ice right below the topsoil on the ground. Only tiny plants can grow, such as lichens and mosses. This area is called tundra.

There is abundant wildlife in the Arctic. There are tons of fish, and many countries harvest fish there. One of the most popular fish is salmon. There are also whales, including the migrating gray whale, which spends its summer in the Arctic. On land, there are arctic hare, foxes, wolves, lemmings, muskox, and caribou that migrate by the thousands across the tundra. The most widely known animal of the Arctic is the polar bear. The polar bear hunts sea animals such as seals on the ice.

Answer the items.

1. If you were to explore the Arctic, what animal would you like to see the most? Tell why.

   _____

2. Do you think the Arctic will change over the next five years? Explain your answer.

   _____

Skill Sharpeners: Geography • EMC 3744 • © Evan-Moor Corp.

ARCTIC
REGION

Aleutian Islands

Kuril Islands   JAPAN

Petropavlovsk-
Kamchatskiy

BERING
SEA

NORTH PACIFIC
OCEAN

Sakhalin

SEA OF
OKHOTSK

Kodiak   Bethel

Providenya   Anadyr   Magadan

Khabarovsk

Amur

Gulf of Alaska   Anchorage
Valdez
Alaska (U.S.)

Arctic Circle

Okhotsk

Kolyma

Whitehorse   Fairbanks
Dawson

CHUKCHI
SEA

Pevek   Cherskiy

Oymyakon   Yakutsk

CHINA

Watson
Lake

Prudhoe
Bay   Barrow

Wrangel Id.

EAST
SIBERIAN
SEA

Verkhoyansk

Aldan

Hay
River

Inuvik

Great Bear
Lake

BEAUFORT
SEA

New
Siberian
Islands

Tiksi

Lena

Yellowknife

Banks
Island

LAPTEV
SEA

CANADA

Victoria
Island

ARCTIC
OCEAN

Lake
Athabasca

Queen
Elizabeth
Islands

RUSSIA

Rankin
Inlet

Hudson
Bay

North
Pole

Severnaya
Zemlya

Norilsk

Yenisey

Ob

Ellesmere
Island

Alert

Franz
Josef
Land

Dikson

KARA
SEA

Qaanaaq
(Thule)

Nord

Novaya
Zemlya

Ob

Iqaluit

Baffin
Bay

Baffin Island

Greenland
(DENMARK)

Longyearbyen

Svalbard
(NORWAY)

BARENTS
SEA

Pechora

Davis Strait

Kangerlussuaq

GREENLAND
SEA

Murmansk

Arkhangelsk

Perm

Severnaya Dvina

Paamiut
Nuuk
(Godthab)

Narsarsuaq   Tasiilaq

Jan Mayen
(NORWAY)

Tromso

Kama

LABRADOR
SEA

Denmark Strait

NORWEGIAN
SEA

Lake
Onega

Kazan

Samara

Arctic Circle

FINLAND

Lake
Ladoga

Nizhniy
Novgorod   Saratov

NORTH ATLANTIC OCEAN

REYKJAVIK   ICELAND

Faroe Islands
(DENMARK)
Torshavn

NORWAY

SWEDEN

HELSINKI
Saint
Petersburg   MOSCOW

Volgograd

KAZ.

Shetland
Islands

OSLO   STOCKHOLM

TALLINN
EST.

Don

Nizhniy

500 km

500 mi

DENMARK

COPENHAGEN

Belfast

IRELAND   U.K.
DUBLIN

NORTH
SEA

RIGA   LAT.

VILNIUS   MINSK
LITH.
RUS.   BELARUS

Kharkiv

Rostov

BERLIN   WARSAW
GERMANY   POLAND

KIEV

UKRAINE

BLACK SEA

Lemming

Muskox

Caribou

Places and Regions

Skill:
Use visual
discrimination

Earth's Poles

Find these words about the North and South Poles in the word search.
Hint: Some are backwards.

shackleton	endurance	antarctica	sailor
south pole	penguin	arctic	tundra
salmon	polar bear	permafrost	

s	a	l	m	o	n	x	f	f	a	x	k	c	t	u
m	y	b	e	s	k	m	x	c	g	z	n	v	l	p
c	w	c	n	c	v	h	i	f	h	o	r	w	h	d
h	b	x	v	p	n	t	d	r	m	e	j	q	e	r
s	k	s	d	f	c	a	h	p	s	f	f	n	s	d
j	h	n	a	r	p	e	r	m	a	f	r	o	s	t
n	p	a	a	i	a	v	h	u	r	c	u	r	u	f
p	k	t	c	f	l	m	h	c	d	t	a	t	n	l
r	n	d	j	k	d	o	i	t	h	n	y	u	i	f
a	z	g	k	u	l	t	r	p	k	w	e	n	u	i
d	h	q	y	u	c	e	o	d	y	s	q	d	g	i
k	h	b	t	r	g	l	t	s	j	p	s	r	n	t
k	k	v	a	t	e	j	o	o	n	q	d	a	e	o
r	a	e	b	r	a	l	o	p	n	w	v	l	p	f
k	z	r	k	f	p	t	p	t	z	d	j	b	i	h

Skill Sharpeners: Geography • EMC 3744 • © Evan-Moor Corp.

Places and Regions

Stuck in the Ice!

Freeze a toy boat in a bowl of ice and observe what happens.

What You Need

- water
- freezer
- large plastic bowl
- plastic toy boat
- various hand tools or utensils

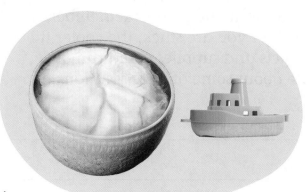

What You Do

1. Fill the plastic bowl two-thirds full with water. Put a plastic boat in the bowl.

2. Place the bowl in the freezer for 4 hours or until the water is completely frozen.

3. Take the bowl out of the freezer. Look at the boat. Is it damaged? When water freezes, it expands, or grows larger. This is what damaged Shackleton's boat when it was stuck in the ice.

4. With help from an adult, see if there are any tools you can use to carefully pry the boat out of the ice. Try to limit the damage to the boat as much as possible.

Places and Regions

Skill:
Write informative text to convey information and experiences clearly

Can You Get Out?

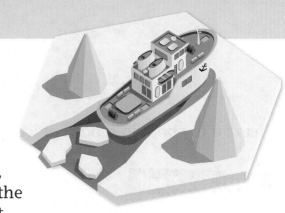

What would you do if your boat was stuck in ice? What special supplies could help you? Remember, the longer you are stuck, the cooler the crew gets and supplies could run out. Write about some of your solutions.

_____

_____

_____

_____

_____

_____

_____

_____

_____

_____

_____

_____

Places and Regions

Thousands of Living Things

Concept:
Different biomes exist on Earth's surface.

My family and I were seated in a meadow in Great Smoky Mountains National Park. We were inspecting the ground for living things. We had been seeing so many bugs and insects all week long. I'll never forget the crazy-colored moths that gathered around the bathrooms' walls at the campground. Or the butterflies that huddled together in clumps.

My sister noticed an orange caterpillar crawling along the ground. "It looks macaroni and cheese colored," she called out. The ranger came over, bent down, and inspected it. "Those are imperial moth caterpillars, one of the thousands of moth and butterfly species in the park."

The ranger took a picture of the brightly colored bug. Then she called everyone over and announced, "Thank you so much for helping identify and count species of living things here in the annual Smokies BioBlitz! Because of volunteers like you, we have added hundreds of creatures to our lists of living things at the park. We didn't even know some of them existed until now! Let's take a break for lunch!"

Everyone began to walk to the picnic area. Suddenly, my sister exclaimed, "Hey, look at this salamander!" We ran over, wondering if she had found another creature to add to our list!

Physical Systems

Concept:
Different biomes exist on Earth's surface.

Plants As Medicine

The word *biodiversity* means "the variety of living things in one area." The Amazon Rainforest of South America is the most biologically diverse place on the planet. It is located close to the equator, so that means the weather there is hot and wet most of the year. It is in parts of nine different countries, including Brazil, Ecuador, and Peru.

The Amazon Rainforest surrounds the Amazon River. There are over 40,000 plant species growing in the Amazon. The Amazon also has the largest variety of tree species growing in the world. In some sections of the rainforest, there are over 100 different types of trees within a very small area of land.

Some of the plants growing in the Amazon are called medicinals. Medicinals are plants used by native people for healing. Modern doctors and scientists are continuing to discover that the Amazon's plants can help with many illnesses. Some of these plants can cure diseases such as malaria, which causes asthma, a condition that makes it difficult to breathe. Many of the medicinals of the Amazon have yet to be discovered by scientists, who are convinced there are more growing in the region.

Answer the items.

1. If the weather in the Amazon changed, do you think the biodiversity would change? Explain your answer.

_____

_____

2. Why do you think scientists are convinced there are more medicinals in the region?

_____

Physical Systems

Skill Sharpeners: Geography • EMC 3744 • © Evan-Moor Corp.

Interior of tropical rainforest in Yasuní National Park, Ecuador

Xylaria telfairii – The liquid inside this fungus is used for earaches by the Quichua Indians in the Ecuadorian Amazon.

Amazon Rainforest in Brazil, South America

Physical Systems

The Amazon

Define It!

canopy: a protective covering of trees and other tall plants

endemic: living only in one location

amphibian: frogs, toads, newts, and salamanders

In the Amazon Rainforest, the trees are so thick that little sunlight reaches the ground. This covering creates the canopy. In and under the canopy are an incredible number of living things. Many of them are endemic, meaning they don't live anywhere else on the planet.

Scientists have counted about 3,000 species of fish in the Amazon. One interesting type is the piranha, which hunts in packs and quickly eats the flesh of its victims.

There are literally thousands of types of insects and spiders in the Amazon. One unique example is leaf-cutter ants. These ants cut up leaves and carry them home over their heads.

The Amazon is also well known for its reptiles and amphibians. Amphibians are frogs, toads, newts, and salamanders. There are about 500 different types of amphibians in the Amazon. One type is the brightly colored poison dart frog. Native people use the poison from its skin to coat their darts or arrowheads when hunting.

There are 1,300 or more different types of birds in the Amazon, too. A famous one is the toucan with its long, colorful beak.

Answer the items.

1. What do you imagine you would see if you sat on the ground in the rainforest?

   _____

2. Do you think the rainforest could be a dangerous place? Explain your answer.

   _____

   _____

Physical Systems

Skill Sharpeners: Geography • EMC 3744 • © Evan-Moor Corp.

piranhas

leaf-cutter ant

poison dart frog

toco toucan

Physical Systems

Amazing Region

The Amazon Rainforest is a unique and amazing place.
Read the description and write the word it describes.

| endemic | medicinals | biodiversity | malaria |
| canopy | species | tropical | |

1. an area that is hot and rainy and near the equator _____

2. the tall covering that rainforest trees create _____

3. living in one certain place or area _____

4. plants used to cure diseases _____

5. a disease spread by mosquitoes _____

6. the variety of living things in an area _____

7. many living things of one type, such as birds _____

Think About It

What is the biodiversity in your area? Make a list of **all** the categories of living things you can think of.

_____

_____

_____

_____

Physical Systems

Do Your Own BioBlitz!

Skill:
Apply geography concepts in context

Observe and document all the living things in a part of your yard or nearby park.

What You Need

- outdoor space
- yardstick or tape measure
- string
- hand lens/magnifying glass

- tweezers or a plastic spoon
- small plastic containers
- paper and pencil
- clock or timer

What You Do

1. Find an outdoor space that has a lot of plants and appears wild.

2. Measure an area 4 feet by 4 feet (1.2 m by 1.2 m). Mark it off with string.

3. Quietly observe all the living things in that area for 30 minutes. List each type of living thing—plants, insects, and anything else you observe.

4. Consider carefully collecting some of the specimens, using tweezers or a plastic spoon and a container. After making your observations, return each specimen to the place you found it.

5. Report your findings of biodiversity to your friends and family.

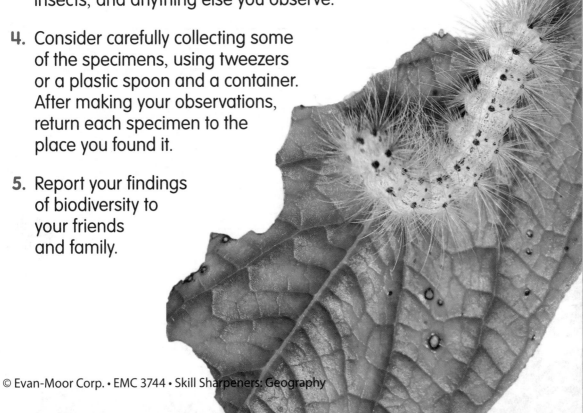

Physical Systems

Tales from the Amazon

Imagine that you had to live in the Amazon Rainforest for one week. What would you see? What would you hear? What would you eat? Write a journal entry about your experiences.

_____

_____

_____

_____

_____

_____

_____

_____

_____

_____

_____

_____

_____

Physical Systems

Skill Sharpeners: Geography • EMC 3744 • © Evan-Moor Corp.

The Dog on the Glacier

Concept:
Physical processes shape features on Earth's surface.

John Muir was a famous explorer. One of the many things he is known for is his interest in glaciers. One such adventure Muir had on a glacier was with his dog, Stickeen, in Alaska in 1880. Muir wrote a book about it entitled *Stickeen*. I saw a reenactment of Muir and Stickeen's adventure. The experience was described like this…

"Stickeen and I had been exploring the Brady Glacier all day. It was getting late and cold and snowy—even though it was summer. We were crossing one crevasse, or deep crack in the ice, after another. Stickeen was doing great. He ran and jumped over each crack easily. Eventually, we came to a crack that was incredibly deep and at least 50 feet wide. We searched up and down for a way to cross. Finally, I found a sliver of an ice bridge and began to make steps in the ice using my ax. As I worked my way down, Stickeen refused to go. He gave me a look as if saying, "Where in the world do you think you are going?" I very carefully stepped from one side of the crevasse to the other. When I got to the other side, Stickeen refused to move. He barked, howled, and whimpered but was too scared to take any steps on the bridge. I didn't know what to do and pleaded with him. I knew there was no way he would survive a night on the glacier. Finally, after I had given up hope, Stickeen jumped, slid, and whizzed past me—on the other side of the crack. It was the happiest moment of my life, and maybe Stickeen's, too, when we were reunited on the other side of the crevasse."

photos courtesy National Park Service

Physical Systems

Glaciers

Concept:
Physical processes shape features on Earth's surface.

John Muir was fascinated by glaciers. There was so much to know about these huge, slowly moving sheets of ice. One of Muir's favorite places to observe glaciers was in California's Sierra Nevada Mountains, in what is now Yosemite National Park.

Muir went to Yosemite in the late 1800s when there were a few small glaciers in the park. Muir noted the features that made them glaciers. They had a crack, or bergschrund, near the top indicating movement. He also observed crevasses, or cracks within the glacier, showing it was moving downhill. Muir saw moraines, or piles of rock, at the base of the glacier, showing where the ice had pushed the rocks forward.

Muir believed that much larger glaciers had once been there. He observed the deep, U-shaped valleys that were carved by huge glaciers in the Ice Age of the past. The Ice Age was a time when Earth was cooler and there were many glaciers. He also saw shiny, polished rocks. He knew that the rocks became shiny because glaciers had moved over them slowly and smoothed them out. In addition, he saw large boulders in places where they could only be by being moved by a glacier. These boulders are called glacial erratics. People continue to learn more about glaciers every day.

Define It!

glacier: a slowly moving field of ice

bergschrund: a large crack near the top of a glacier

moraine: a pile of rocks a glacier pushes ahead of it

glacial erratic: a boulder moved by a glacier and left there

Answer the item.

Can anyone prove that a glacier moves? Explain your answer.

_____

_____

_____

_____

Physical Systems

Skill Sharpeners: Geography • EMC 3744 • © Evan-Moor Corp.

Half Dome in Yosemite National Park, California

Glacial erratic boulder at Olmsted Point in Yosemite National Park

El Capitan and Bridalveil Fall in Yosemite National Park in the western Sierra Nevada mountains

Physical Systems

Concept:
Physical processes shape features on Earth's surface.

Europe's Glaciers

Europe has many glaciers. One reason for this is that there are very high mountains in Europe, including the Alps. High mountains lead to colder weather and more snow. Also, much of Europe is far north in latitude, which makes the weather cooler.

Define It!

Alps: a high mountain range in Europe

latitude: measured distance from the equator

climate change: warmer weather occurring on Earth due, in part, to human activities

Some European countries with glaciers include Switzerland, Austria, Germany, France, and Italy. Europe's largest glacier, though, is in Norway. The Jostedalsbreen Glacier in Norway is 37 miles (60 km) long and 2,000 feet (610 m) thick.

Most of Europe's glaciers are melting because of climate change. In some European locations, countries are trying to slow down glacier melt by covering them with huge white cloths or blankets. White is used because it reflects the sun. The glaciers are also being covered to help prevent ski resorts from losing business due to shorter seasons. Also, towns below the glaciers depend on the glacial ice melting slowly as a consistent water source. Slowing down the melt of the glacier ensures that these towns will have the glacier's water longer.

Answer the item.

What else do you think could be done to protect the glaciers in Europe?

_____

_____

_____

Grandes Jorasses and Aiguille du Midi
Mountains in the French Alps

Melting Rhone Glacier
in Switzerland – View
from Furka Pass

Jostedalsbreen
Glacier in
Norway

Physical Systems

49

Glacier Words

Find these glacier words in the word search.
Hint: Some are backwards.

moraine   bergschrund   alps   latitude

glacier   climate change   muir

Physical Systems

Skill Sharpeners: Geography • EMC 3744 • © Evan-Moor Corp.

Protecting the Ice

Skill:
Apply geography concepts in context

Try an experiment to see if covering ice really slows its melting!

What You Need

- water
- two large plastic bowls
- freezer
- white towel or cloth

What You Do

1. Fill the plastic bowls two-thirds full of water. Place both bowls in the freezer overnight so that the water freezes solid.

2. Take out both bowls and place them in a sunny place. Cover the ice in one of the bowls with the white towel.

3. Observe both bowls to see which "glacier" melts the fastest!

Physical Systems

Glacier Protection

Covering a glacier is one way to preserve it, or make it last longer. But the real problem is global warming. Can you think of a way to slow down or stop global warming from melting glaciers completely? Write about your ideas.

_____

_____

_____

_____

_____

_____

_____

_____

_____

_____

_____

Physical Systems

Concept:
Different biomes exist on Earth's surface.

The Hall of Mosses

Earlier today I was in an incredibly unusual place. After my visit, I pulled out my journal and wrote about my experience…

We were on a guided walk on the Hall of Mosses Trail in Olympic National Park in Washington. The ranger told us that this part of the park is wetter than almost any other place in the United States. It gets 140 to 170 inches (356 to 432 cm) of rain a year! The whole area, she said, is a temperate rainforest. The trees grow in incredibly thick. Mosses and ferns were growing everywhere. It was like a jungle, and there was hardly any sun getting through. Looking around, I saw fallen trees that had plants and new trees growing out of them. The ranger said that some of the trees were conifers, meaning they would stay green all year. One type of tree, the Sitka spruce, was one of the largest anywhere. Others were deciduous, like the big leaf maple. She said it would lose its leaves in the fall.

Finally, we got to the destination spot of the trail—the Hall of Mosses. The dense trees were draped in a thick coat of moss. The ranger said that some of the plants don't even need soil to grow on. They sprout right out of other plants. It certainly was unlike any place I had ever seen before.

Physical Systems

Temperate Rainforests

Define It!

conifers: trees that stay green all year

deciduous: trees that lose their leaves in fall

epiphyte: a plant that grows harmlessly on another plant

The Olympic Rainforest in Washington is a temperate rainforest. This means the forest has warm, mostly dry summers, but long, cool, and wet winters. Temperate rainforests are mostly located in what is called the "Roaring 40s" latitude zone. This part of the Earth gets strong winds that drive storms toward land. Also, the inland mountains block the storms, making them drop extra rain on the forest. The trees are a mix of conifers and deciduous. Some plants are epiphytes—they grow right off other plants. Some fallen trees become nurse logs, meaning other plants and trees sprout right on the logs and grow from them. Temperate rainforests occur in only a few parts of the Earth. Some well-known temperate rainforests are on the west coast of the United States from Northern California to Alaska. They are also in western New Zealand's South Island and in Tasmania of Australia. Norway, Peru, and Argentina also have small strips of temperate rainforests.

Answer the items.

1. How would you describe a temperate rainforest?

   _____

   _____

2. What part of the temperate rainforest interests you the most?

   _____

   _____

Physical Systems

Epiphytic fern and fresh green peat moss growing on a nurse log

Nurse log in Olympic National Park, Washington

Decaying stump, known as a nurse stump, with a new tree growing out of the old one

Physical Systems

Gondwana

Define It!

endemic: growing or living nowhere else

endangered: a plant or an animal that has very few left alive

marsupial: an animal with a pouch for its young

On New Zealand's South Island, a large area of temperate rainforest is preserved in five different national parks. There are many types of plants, animals, and birds living there. One special bird is the takahē. This flightless bird is endemic, which means it lives nowhere else on the planet. It is about the size of a chicken and runs on its short, strong legs. The bird is also endangered, but its numbers are increasing.

In Tasmania, an island south of Australia's mainland, there are also sections of protected temperate rainforest. Australia's temperate rainforest has an incredible variety of living species. One reason for this is the Australian continent used to be part of a supercontinent called Gondwana. Millions of years ago, most landmasses in the Southern Hemisphere were merged together as one big continent. Plant and animal species developed on Gondwana until the plates fractured and began drifting apart. Now, species related to that period of time live in isolated areas, including Tasmania. One unique animal is the Tasmanian devil. This carnivorous, or meat-eating, marsupial lives only in Tasmania.

Answer the items.

1. In your own words, describe what a takahē bird looks like.

_____

2. Explain how the different species on Tasmania became isolated.

_____

_____

Takahē, once thought to be extinct, in Fiordland National Park, South Island

Tasmanian devil

McLean Falls in Catlins Forest Park, South New Zealand

Physical Systems

Skill:
Apply content
vocabulary in
context

Special Rainforests

Read the description and write the word it describes.

nurse log	marsupial	deciduous	endemic
hemisphere	temperate	conifer	epiphyte

1. a tree that remains green all year _____

2. plants sprout right on this log _____

3. a plant that grows on another plant _____

4. an animal that has a pouch for its young _____

5. one section of Earth divided in half _____

6. a plant or an animal that lives only in
   a certain area _____

7. a rainforest that has a dry summer
   and a long, wet winter _____

8. trees that lose their leaves in fall _____

Think About It

Do you think Earth's landmasses are still moving? If so, tell
where you think they might be millions of years from now.

_____

_____

_____

Physical Systems

Skill Sharpeners: Geography • EMC 3744 • © Evan-Moor Corp.

Create a Nurse Log

Skill:
Apply geography concepts in context

Try to grow a plant from seed on a nurse log.

What You Need

- decaying wood stump, branch, or wood chips
- water
- seeds of various types
- outside area

What You Do

1. Find a decaying piece of wood. It should appear to be falling apart. Wood chips may be used as an alternative.

2. Place the wood in a cool, wet outdoor location to simulate the rainforest. Wet the wood several times a day for a few days.

3. Scatter several types of seeds over the wood. Water it lightly and often to keep the wood moist.

4. Observe the wood over a period of a few weeks to see if it acts like a nurse log and the seeds sprout. If so, keep them alive and growing!

Physical Systems

Skill:
Write to
persuade

Save the Temperate Rainforests

People are trying to cut down the temperate rainforests. Write a persuasive letter to save them. Include details about the locations and the importance of temperate rainforests.

_____

_____

_____

_____

_____

_____

_____

_____

_____

_____

_____

_____

Physical Systems

60

Concept:
Human settlements and archaeological remains illustrate human imprints on the physical environment.

Saturday Explorations

My mom is an archaeologist. She studies artifacts from past civilizations. Mom specializes in learning about Native Americans from the desert southeast of the United States.

We live in Phoenix, Arizona, smack dab in the desert. It is very hot here in the summer. But when the weather cools, Mom takes me out to explore with her.

Hundreds of years ago, the Anasazi and Navajo peoples lived in the area I live in now. They built stone homes, grew crops, stored food, and made tools such as arrowheads.

Saturday mornings we often drive out to a canyon somewhere in Arizona or Utah. We find a dry wash, or where water sometimes runs through. Then we grab our tools—mostly just small hand shovels and a sieve, or sifter. We go to the dry creek, scoop up some sand and rock, and pour it through the sieve. It takes time and patience. But Mom knows exactly where to look.

You should see our collection at home. We have many artifacts, including arrowheads, but also broken pieces of ancient pottery. Most of our finds have been shipped off to museums where they belong. That's where Mom works, too. And that is what I want to do when I grow up—just what Mom does!

Human Systems

Ancient Greece

Human Systems

Define It!

artifact: an item from a past civilization

architecture: designing and creating buildings

excavation: where past ruins are dug up

debitage: stone flakes or chips left over from tools made

Greece is one of the best places in Europe and in the entire world to see artifacts. The ancient Greeks had a strong interest in art, architecture, which is all about designing and constructing buildings, science, and math. The artifacts discovered in Greece are 2,000 to 4,000 years old.

Greece has many excavation sites where archaeologists and researchers have dug up and restored or preserved ruins. Some of the best places include Asprochaliko, where half a million flaked stone tools and debitage, or stone fragments left over from tool making, have been found. In Epidaurus, an ancient theatre was built that is still in use today. Crete has palaces and cities preserved from dig sites. In Delphi, there are ancient buildings and temples. And Olympia has ruins preserved from the first Olympic Games, which started in Greece in 776 BCE. Today, the Olympic torch is lit at a temple there and then transported to wherever the Olympic Games are being held.

Answer the items.

1. Why do you think math was an important part of ancient Greek civilizations?

   _____

   _____

   _____

2. What do the number of archaeological sites in Greece tell you about Greek life?

   _____

   _____

FYROM

BULGARIA

ALBANIA

Kavala • Komotini

Edessa • Thessaloniki

Ioannina Larissa   TURKEY

Corfu
Corfu   Volos   Lemnos

Preveza   Lamia   Aegean   Lesbos
                        Sea

Cephalonia   Patras

Olympia   ATHENS

Sparta   CYCLADES

Cythera   Sea of Crete   Rhodes

                        Karpathos

Heraklion

Crete

Mediterranean Sea

**Ancient ruins of the Philippeion in Olympia,
Greece – birthplace of the Olympic Games**

**Ancient Epidaurus Theatre
in Argolida, Greece**

Human Systems

How Old Is It?

Concept:

Human settlements and archaeological remains illustrate human imprints on the physical environment.

Human Systems

Define It!

archaeologist: someone who studies ancient civilizations

carbon: an element in all living things

decay: to break down or fall apart over time

Archaeologists find artifacts all over the world. In doing so, they learn about how people lived and what their beliefs may have been.

Archaeologists often make surprising discoveries. For example, 100,000-year-old shells used as jewelry were discovered at Skhul Cave in Israel. At Sibudu Cave in South Africa, archaeologists found tools that were 77,000 years old. The world's oldest bow, as used for hunting with a bow and arrow, was found in Denmark. It is estimated to be 8,000 years old.

There are several ways archaeologists date how old an item is. One is to carefully examine the rock layer the artifact was found in. Scientists can determine how old the soil is and relate the soil's age to the item. Archaeologists can also compare artifacts to each other to determine how old they are. Another way to determine the age of an item is radiocarbon dating. Carbon is an element in all living things. As living things die and decay, they release carbon. The carbon they release is at a constant rate and at set amounts. So scientists can measure how much carbon is left in an item and determine how old the artifact is.

Answer the items.

1. Which method would you use to determine how old an artifact is? Explain why.

   _____

2. Do you think there are more artifacts to be discovered? Why haven't people found all of them yet?

   _____

Skill Sharpeners: Geography • EMC 3744 • © Evan-Moor Corp.

Skhul Cave on Mount Carmel in Israel

Researchers at Atapuerca site in Spain – Fossils and stone tools of the earliest known humans in West Europe were found here.

Ancient ceramic shards from different epochs, or periods, of Israel history

Human Systems

Skill:
Apply content vocabulary

Exploring the Past

Solve this crossword puzzle with words about the past.

debitage	architecture	decay	greece
museum	archaeologist	artifact	carbon

Across

2. person who studies the past and its items
4. natural element that is released by an object once it dies
5. item from the distant past
6. to break down over time
7. chips of stone left over from tool making

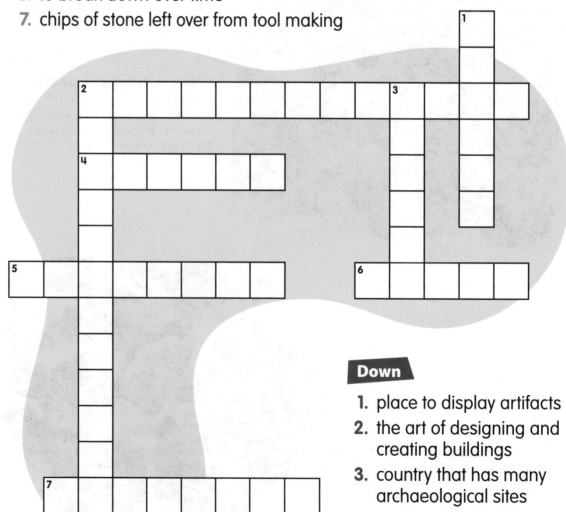

Down

1. place to display artifacts
2. the art of designing and creating buildings
3. country that has many archaeological sites

Human Systems

Artifacts at Home

Invite your friends over to view artifacts from your home.

What You Need

- five or more "old" items from your home

What You Do

1. Ask your parents for five or more of the oldest items in your home. Make sure that you treat each item carefully.

2. Learn as much as you can about each item. Try to learn the item's age, origin (where it came from), and what it was used for.

3. Invite your friends to your home for a show-and-tell session. Tell them what you know about each artifact. Talk about how modern-day items are similar to or different from the artifacts.

Human Systems

Protecting the Past

Imagine that you just discovered an
ancient artifact. You will excavate it,
or dig it out, and send it to a museum.
Draw a picture of the artifact and explain
where you found it, what you think it is,
and how old it might be.

_____

_____

_____

_____

_____

_____

_____

Skill:
Write narrative
text about real-
world situations

Human Systems

Scouting the Globe

Concept:
Connections between cultures lead to cultural change.

My aunt is a scout for a Major League Baseball team. She travels throughout the United States and to other countries looking for players to recruit. My aunt says that there are talented players all over the world, it's just a matter of finding them. She says that baseball used to be thought of as an American sport. But now it is definitely thought of as an international sport.

Once in a while, I get to go with her on her travels. We drive to baseball games and write notes about the players. We also video record them in action. Then my aunt sends the information to the team managers. Her hope is that they will sign a player to a contract. That's the exciting part—and, of course, seeing a player make it to the Major Leagues. My aunt says that baseball was a difficult sport for her to break in to. She's one of the few female baseball scouts in the world. I think every person should be allowed to show how great he or she is at his or her job, so I'm glad my aunt was given a chance to prove herself.

Tomorrow we are going to see a pitcher who is in the Minor Leagues. My aunt says that he is from the Dominican Republic. The day after that, we are going to see a high school student from Kansas. People say that he can hit a home run five days a week!

I hope that I can be a scout like my aunt when I grow up. I like the idea of looking for talented players. I also like the idea of helping my aunt change the world—I'm a girl, too.

Human Systems

Spanning the Globe

Concept:
Connections between cultures lead to cultural change.

Human Systems

Define It!

MLB: Major League Baseball

professional: highly skilled

scout: a person who searches for talented ball players

Baseball is often called "America's Sport." The United States has two Major League Baseball (MLB) divisions: the American League and the National League. Many players in these leagues are from the United States. However, several players are from other countries, including Australia, Canada, Cuba, the Dominican Republic, Japan, Mexico, Puerto Rico, South Korea, and Venezuela.

Baseball leagues have become popular around the world. Countries such as Japan, Australia, Israel, Cuba, and China, among other places, all have professional baseball leagues. Major League scouts from the United States watch players from other leagues. A foreign player can come into MLB by being scouted. Ichiro Suzuki from Japan is one example. He played for years in Japan then came to the United States. He is considered one of the greatest hitters of all time, and he recently made his 3,000th hit in MLB.

MLB sometimes plays games overseas. They have played in Mexico, Japan, Australia, and Puerto Rico. So, the next time you sing "Take Me Out to the Ball Game," remember that this song is sung worldwide!

Answer the items.

1. Why do you think so many countries started professional baseball leagues?

   _____

2. Do you think having teams all over the world helps the sport become more popular? Explain your answer.

   _____

Skill Sharpeners: Geography • EMC 3744 • © Evan-Moor Corp.

Ichiro Suzuki, right fielder for the Seattle Mariners, hits during a game against the Cleveland Indians at Progressive Field in Ohio, 2012

Jorge Bonifacio, right fielder for the Kansas City Royals, hits during a game against the San Francisco Giants at AT&T Park in California, 2017

Ichiro Suzuki, right fielder for the Seattle Mariners, at bat during a game against the Oakland Athletics at the Coliseum in California, 2010

Human Systems

Concept:
Connections between cultures lead to cultural change.

Negro Leagues

Professional baseball leagues have existed since the late 1800s. Because of discrimination, African American players were not welcome to play on Major League Baseball teams. In 1920, African Americans formed the Negro National League. They played in the United States, Canada, and sometimes Latin America.

In 1945, Jackie Robinson was recruited from the Kansas City Monarchs, a Negro League team, into Major League Baseball. Robinson joined the Brooklyn Dodgers in 1947, becoming the first African American to play in MLB.

In 1960, the Negro Leagues came to an end as many of their best players were recruited into the Major Leagues. While this was a great opportunity for the players, it was not without its challenges and struggles. Two of the Negro Leagues' most famous players were:

Satchel Paige: He was a pitcher for the Monarchs from 1926 until 1947. At 42 years old, he made it into the Major Leagues and played for 6 years. He also played one year at age 59!

Josh Gibson: He played in the Negro Leagues for 16 years and hit 800 home runs! He was a catcher, and he is thought of as the best hitter of all time in the Negro Leagues.

Answer the item.

Do you think a person's ethnicity should matter when it comes to playing a sport? Explain your answer.

_____

_____

Human Systems

Jackie Robinson wearing a Dodgers uniform, 1954

Human Systems

Skill:
Apply content
vocabulary

Baseball Around the World

Solve this crossword puzzle with words about baseball.

dodgers	international	suzuki
gibson	jackie robinson	scout
paige	professional	recruit

Down

1. including countries from all over the world
3. team that signed Jackie Robinson
4. famous player from Japan
6. pitcher in Negro Leagues and MLB
7. hit 800 home runs

Across

2. highly skilled
5. person who searches for talented ball players
8. first African American player in the Major Leagues
9. to enlist a person to work for you

Human Systems

Skill Sharpeners: Geography • EMC 3744 • © Evan-Moor Corp.

Mapping the Players

Map where your favorite baseball team's players are from.

What You Need

- world map
- Internet access
- colored pins or tacks

Yu Darvish

Position: Pitcher
Bats: Right • **Throws:** Right
6' 5", 220 lb (196 cm, 99 kg)
Team: Los Angeles Dodgers (Majors)
Born: August 16, 1986 in Habikino, Japan
High School: Tohoku (Sendai, Japan)

What You Do

1. Pick your favorite MLB team. Look up where ten of your favorite players are from on that team. Complete player profiles and information can be found at: http://www.baseball-reference.com

2. Label the world map with pins or tacks showing where each of your favorite players are from. Next to each tack or pin, write the player's name and any other information you'd like.

3. Show your international baseball map to your family and friends.

Human Systems

Baseball Connections

Can people learn about different cultures by watching or playing a sport? Do you think the game of baseball helps connect people from around the world? Write your opinions to answer these questions.

_____

_____

_____

_____

_____

_____

_____

_____

_____

_____

_____

_____

_____

_____

Human Systems

Concept:
Countries cooperate to manage resources and solve human issues.

Lost and Found

It is time for my family's annual trip to New Zealand. We go for two weeks each January, which is our winter and their summer. This makes sense because New Zealand is in the Southern Hemisphere. We love to go sightseeing in Auckland, New Zealand's largest city. However, sometimes it takes us a few days to adjust to the time difference. Check this out…

Our flight is scheduled to leave Los Angeles, California, at 10:30 p.m. in the evening. We fly about 13 hours directly to Sydney, Australia, and have a few hours layover. Then we board our next flight to Auckland. That one takes 4 hours before we arrive at our final destination. All in all, it's about 21 hours travel time, but it's two days later if you are looking at a calendar. We actually lose two days instead of one because of the time zones across the globe. Needless to say, we all end up with quite a bit of jet lag.

Coming home is a completely different story. Now we fly in reverse from Auckland to Sydney to Los Angeles. The entire trip home takes around 20 hours. But here's the weird part—we arrive at the same time we left because the time zones change in reverse! So, some of the time that was lost is found!

You'd think after all that travel, looking at a clock would make us dizzy. It takes us a few days to get our bearings back.

11:30 a.m. Saturday, leave Auckland

12:30 p.m. Saturday, arrive Los Angeles

Human Systems

Time Zones

Concept:
Countries cooperate to manage resources and solve human issues.

Define It!

rotate: to spin around in a circle

time zones: 24 sections of Earth with different times

zenith: when the sun is at its highest point, directly overhead

The Earth spins every day, making a complete rotation in 24 hours. The 24 hours it takes the Earth to do this is called a day. If there was only one time over all of Earth every day, some areas would be light and others would be dark. As the Earth rotates, a section moves into the sunlight. This is called sunrise. As that section of the Earth rotates away from the sun, it gets dark. This is called evening.

In order to make some sense of this, times zones were created in the 1800s. The whole Earth is divided into 24 of them. The mean or base time zone is in Greenwich, England, at the prime meridian. Each time zone is measured in 15-degree sections from the prime meridian. All the way around the Earth is 360 degrees. When you divide 360 by 15 degrees, that makes 24, or 24 hours in a day. This way everyone on Earth gets sunlight much more evenly!

The 24 time zones assure that every section or place on the globe gets a zenith time of day, which is at 12 o'clock noon.

Answer the items.

1. Look at the clocks that show the different times zones for 24 cities. Do you see any patterns in how the times change?

   _____

   _____

   _____

2. Do you think the way the time zones are divided makes sense?

   _____

   _____

Human Systems

Skill Sharpeners: Geography • EMC 3744 • © Evan-Moor Corp.

These clocks show the time in different cities in each of the 24 time zones on Earth.

10 pm
Pago Pago

11 pm
Kiritimati

12 am
Honolulu

01 am
Anchorage

02 am
Vancouver

03 am
Mexico City

04 am
Boston

05 am
Montevideo

06 am
Nuuk

07 am
Praia

08 am
Dakar

09 am
London

10 am
Madrid

11 am
Athens

12:30 pm
Kabul

01 pm
Karachi

1:45 pm
Kathmandu

03 pm
Bangkok

04 pm
Hong Kong

05 pm
Tokyo

06 pm
Sydney

07 pm
Honiara

08 pm
Auckland

09 pm
Nuku'alufa

Human Systems

What Time Is It?

Concept:
Countries cooperate to manage resources and solve human issues.

Define It!

time zone: one of 24 time locations on Earth

noncontiguous: in close proximity without actually touching

mainland: main part of the United States

The United States has six time zones in all. Two time zones are in the noncontiguous United States. They are Hawaii–Aleutian time and Alaska time. There are four time zones in the mainland United States. Going from west to east, the time zones are called Pacific, mountain, central, and eastern. Each of these time zones is one hour later than the previous one. If it is 1:00 p.m. Pacific time, it is 2:00 p.m. mountain time, 3:00 p.m. central time, and 4:00 p.m. eastern time.

The time zones in the mainland United States are usually determined by the state's borders. However, there are 14 different states that are in two time zones. For example, most of Idaho is in the mountain time zone. But northwest Idaho is in the Pacific time zone. That part of the state is close to Spokane, Washington, the nearest large city in the Pacific time zone. So, people in northwest Idaho's small cities follow the time of Spokane. This is done to make it easier to work with businesses and schools.

Answer the items.

1. Have you ever changed time zones when you traveled? Did it affect your sleep?

_____

_____

2. Do you think having different time zones makes things easier or more difficult?

_____

_____

Skill Sharpeners: Geography • EMC 3744 • © Evan-Moor Corp.

Human Systems

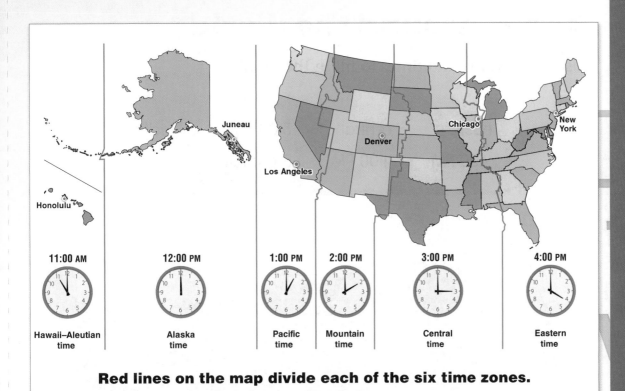

11:00 AM Hawaii–Aleutian time

12:00 PM Alaska time

1:00 PM Pacific time

2:00 PM Mountain time

3:00 PM Central time

4:00 PM Eastern time

Red lines on the map divide each of the six time zones.

Human Systems

Skill:
Apply content
vocabulary in
context

Times Around the World

Use these words and times to fill in the blanks.

eastern	central	3:00 PM	Pacific
2:00 PM	4:00 PM	mountain	

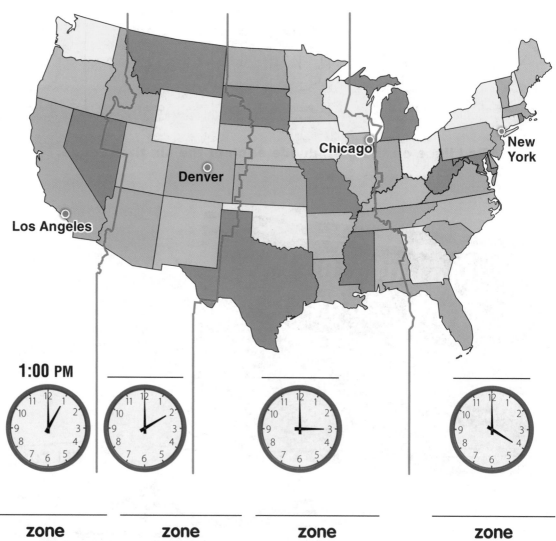

1:00 PM

zone   **zone**   **zone**   **zone**

Human Systems

Planning a Trip

Plan a trip to destinations in different time zones.

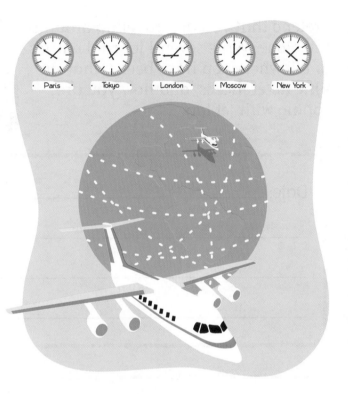

What You Need

- Internet access
- paper
- pencil or pen
- world map

What You Do

1. Choose a major city near you with an airport. Mark this on the map as your starting point.

2. Choose a destination to fly to. Make sure the destination is in another time zone. Mark it on the map.

3. Now choose a second destination to fly to, once again, in a new time zone. Mark it on the map.

4. Choose your third and final destination, mark it, and then fly home to your starting point.

5. Do some research to see how long it takes to fly to each destination you chose. Then write what time (and day, if necessary) you will arrive in each location based on your starting point time being 12:00 p.m. (noon).

6. Share your travel plans with your family.

Skill:
Apply geography concepts in real-world situations

Human Systems

Oh, the Places I Will Go!

Pretend that you are traveling around the globe. Write several journal entries to tell where you have been, what the time difference is, and how you are coping with jet lag.

Date: _____

_____

_____

_____

Date: _____

_____

_____

_____

Date: _____

_____

_____

_____

Human Systems

84

Concept:
Settlements are established where locations provide opportunities.

A Secret Journey

Let's go on a secret journey deep into the wilderness in the desert southwest of the United States. We'll hike several miles until we come to a river. From there we'll climb steep hills until we reach an ancient ladder built by Anasazi Native Americans, or Ancestral Puebloans. At the top of the ladder, we'll squeeze our way through a window in the rocks. Then we'll enter a mysterious lost world. What we have entered is an ancient cliff dwelling built by the Anasazi who lived there 1,000 years ago.

The room is littered with their supplies. There are arrowheads, pieces of broken pottery and bowls, and drawings etched into the ceiling of the room. Our greatest discovery, though? An ancient bowl full of seeds!

The Anasazi left the area about 800 years ago because of a severe drought. Without water, they could no longer plant or grow crops or find game. Their springs were dry. The seeds they left behind we'll be able to take home and plant. That's because my mom is a professor and has a permit to study the area. Months later we'll have stalks of edible squash to eat, all from seeds 800 years old. The place where all this took place is a secret. If people knew the location, Mom says, it would get ruined, so I have told you all I can. Sorry!

Human Systems

A Giant Well

Concept:
Settlements are established where locations provide opportunities.

Define It!

sinkhole: a collapsed area of rock

well: an inground source for water

canal: a man-made channel for water

drought: a long period with little rainfall

Water has always been scarce for people living in a desert. Despite that fact, native peoples dwelled for over 10,000 years in the Verde Valley of northern Arizona. They built homes, hunted, and grew crops smack dab in the desert.

Their secret? A giant sinkhole, or collapsed area, of limestone rock that became a natural well. It is still fed today by an underground spring that provides over a million gallons a day. As far back as the 8th century, people used the water for irrigation. They built a series of canals up to 7 miles (11 km) long. These canals helped people grow crops and take care of other domestic uses, such as drinking and bathing. This allowed people to thrive in the area despite persistent droughts that occurred because creeks would stop flowing.

Near the well, about 800 to 1,000 years ago, the Sinagua Native Americans built a five-story structure high atop a cliff with over twenty rooms. That structure is well-preserved today and is called Montezuma Castle. About 350,000 people a year visit the castle and other nearby ruins.

Answer the items.

1. Why do you think people built Montezuma Castle high off the ground?

   _____

   _____

2. Montezuma Castle has been described as "amazing." Do you agree? Why or why not?

   _____

   _____

Human Systems

Skill Sharpeners: Geography • EMC 3744 • © Evan-Moor Corp.

Montezuma Well National Monument

Canal from Montezuma Well

Montezuma Castle National Monument protects a set of well-preserved Sinaguan cliff dwellings in Camp Verde, Arizona.

Human Systems

Concept:
Settlements are established where locations provide opportunities.

Roman Water

Define It!

aqueduct: a man-made waterway

wastewater: used, dirty water

drainage: a way of moving used water away from an area

About 2,400 years ago, ancient Romans built aqueducts to move water from distant places into their cities. The aqueducts were channels constructed of concrete, stone, or brick. Some were multiple levels built above the ground to carry water across flat valleys. Once the water was in the cities, pipes were used to guide the water throughout the area for public use. Some of the water went to bath houses, which were common in ancient Rome. Cities also had fountains where people could go to get their water.

Some of the water became wastewater and had to be moved out of the city. The Romans set up drainage systems that guided the used water downhill toward the Tiber River, where it was dumped. The main drainage system constructed in ancient Rome is still in use today, as are some of the aqueducts for moving water into the city. The ancient Roman water system was considered quite advanced for the time, and over one million people benefited from it.

Answer the items.

1. Why do you think the ancient Roman water system was considered advanced for the time?

   _____

   _____

2. How many men do you think it took to built the aqueducts? Explain your answer.

   _____

   _____

Human Systems

Roman Pont du Gard aqueduct crossing the Garden River in southern France – a UNESCO World Heritage site

First Roman waterworks system in Ancient Corinth, Greece

Human Systems

Skill:
Apply content vocabulary in context

Is There Enough Water?

Read the description and write the word it describes.

well	sinkhole	irrigation	canal
drought	domestic	wastewater	drainage

1. a man-made channel for moving water _____

2. used water that is no longer clean _____

3. moving water from one place to another to water crops _____

4. a collapsed area of land _____

5. a hole in the earth that provides a supply of water _____

6. the act of removing used water from an area _____

7. a long period of time with little rainfall _____

8. a part of everyday life in a home _____

Think About It

Everyone needs water. What are some ways to help save water or make the water you have last longer?

_____

_____

_____

_____

Human Systems

Skill:
Apply geography concepts

Montezuma Castle

Use sand to make a miniature model of Montezuma Castle.

What You Need

- large area of sand
- twigs or sticks (for tools)
- water
- trowel

What You Do

1. Study the pictures of Montezuma Castle.

2. After reviewing the pictures, make a miniature model of the Montezuma Castle site in the sand. Use sand, water, and twigs or sticks to help re-create the castle.

3. Once you have your model ready, show it to someone and explain what it is and its history.

Human Systems

Changing the Land

The ancient Romans built aqueducts. The Sinagua peoples built Montezuma Castle. How did their actions change the land? Do you think they made positive changes? Write about it.

_____

_____

_____

_____

_____

_____

_____

_____

_____

_____

_____

_____

_____

_____

_____

Human Systems

Concept:
People use technology to get what they need from the physical environment.

The Mighty Colorado

I had to give a speech about the Colorado River to my class. This is what I said: *"If you followed a drop of water on the Colorado River, you would go on quite a journey. Snow melts high up in the Rocky Mountains, and that is where the river starts. It travels 1,450 miles (2,334 km) through seven states and into Mexico. At first the river grows larger and larger as more melted snow feeds it and its tributaries, or other rivers add water to it. It flows out of the mountains and through canyons with rapids. The river pours into Lake Powell, then cuts right between the Grand Canyon and into man-made Lake Mead near Las Vegas, Nevada. After that, it continues flowing along the California and Arizona border and into Baja California, which is Mexico.*

Along the way, people have built dams, reservoirs, and aqueducts. Water is taken out of the Colorado River in many places and is used to serve millions of people in towns and cities. Farms use the water for crops. There are also hydroelectric plants along the Colorado for making electricity. When the Colorado River reaches the ocean in Baja California, it is a slow-moving trickle of its former self." I made one last statement: *"The Colorado River is a very important river. But people have changed it quite a bit."*

I finished my speech and showed pictures of the Colorado River. From its cold beginnings in the mountains and all the way to its end, where it is barely moving. *"Any questions?"* I asked.

Environment and Society

Panama Canal

Environment and Society

Another area of controlled water is the Panama Canal. Panama is a small, narrow country in Central America. It connects North and South America. Since the age of great ocean explorers in the 1500s, there was talk about connecting the Atlantic and Pacific Oceans through the Isthmus of Panama. An isthmus is a thin strip of land with a large sea or ocean on either side. Ships had to go all the way around South America, passing through the Strait of Magellan. It was a long and difficult journey, taking 3 to 6 months. The Strait of Magellan is known for its treacherous high waves, storms, and strong winds.

France began work on the Panama Canal in 1881. But work on the project was stopped in 1889 due to torrential rains, landslides, and tropical diseases carried by mosquitoes.

The United States took over in 1904. They used the military to help out, as well as mosquito-control techniques. When the U.S. finished the canal in 1914, it was the most expensive project they had ever completed.

Tens of thousands of freighters, or ships carrying goods, now travel through the canal, saving months of ocean journey. Ocean travel from the Atlantic Ocean to the Pacific Ocean can now be completed in 6 to 8 hours.

Answer the items.

1. Why was the Panama Canal built?

   _____

   _____

2. What did the United States do to successfully complete the canal?

   _____

   _____

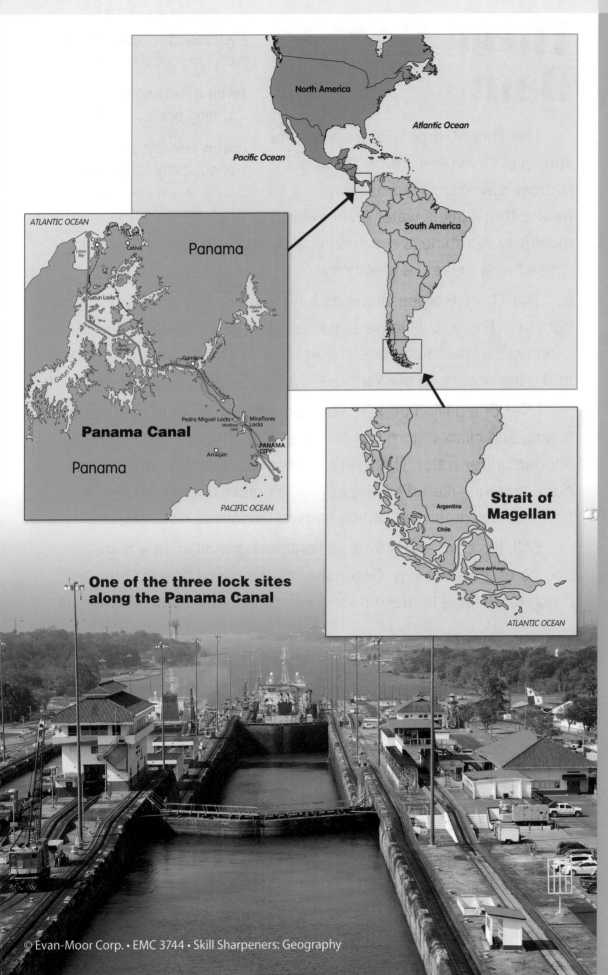

North America

Atlantic Ocean

Pacific Ocean

South America

ATLANTIC OCEAN

Colón   Cativá

Limon Bay

Panama

Gatun Locks

Alajuela Lake

Barro Colorado Isl.

Gamboa

Pedro Miguel Locks   Miraflores Locks

Miraflores Lake

Panama Canal

Arraiján   PANAMA CITY

Panama

PACIFIC OCEAN

Argentina   **Strait of Magellan**

Chile

Tierra del Fuego

ATLANTIC OCEAN

One of the three lock sites along the Panama Canal

© Evan-Moor Corp. • EMC 3744 • Skill Sharpeners: Geography

Environment and Society

Three Gorges Dam

Concept:
People use technology to get what they need from the physical environment.

Define It!

hydroelectric: using moving water to produce electricity

turbine: an engine with spinning blades inside it

green energy: power without using fossil fuels

The Three Gorges Dam and power station in China is the world's largest hydroelectric dam. *Hydroelectric* means that it takes water and moves it through turbines to create electricity. A turbine is a mechanical device with blades that spin, which helps make the electricity.

The Three Gorges Dam has a huge reservoir, or area of water, behind it. This allows large ships called freighters to sail into inland China rather than just dock at ports. The dam also controls flooding that often occurs on the Yangtze River.

Over one million people were forced to move from their homes, towns, and cities before the dam was built. These areas are now flooded under water. The river's course was changed due to the dam, and this altered fishing as well as other habitats. The water flow was also changed, which causes landslides downstream.

Still, the dam and power station have given China a huge source of green energy. *Green* means they don't have to burn as much fossil fuels to make power. Fossil fuels are coal, oil, and gas.

Answer the items.

1. What are some benefits of the Three Gorges Dam?

   _____

   _____

2. What are some problems the dam has caused?

   _____

   _____

Environment and Society

Skill Sharpeners: Geography • EMC 3744 • © Evan-Moor Corp.

Ship entering the first lock at the Three Gorges Dam – Smaller ships use the newer ship lift, which cuts the trip to 40 minutes instead of 3 hours.

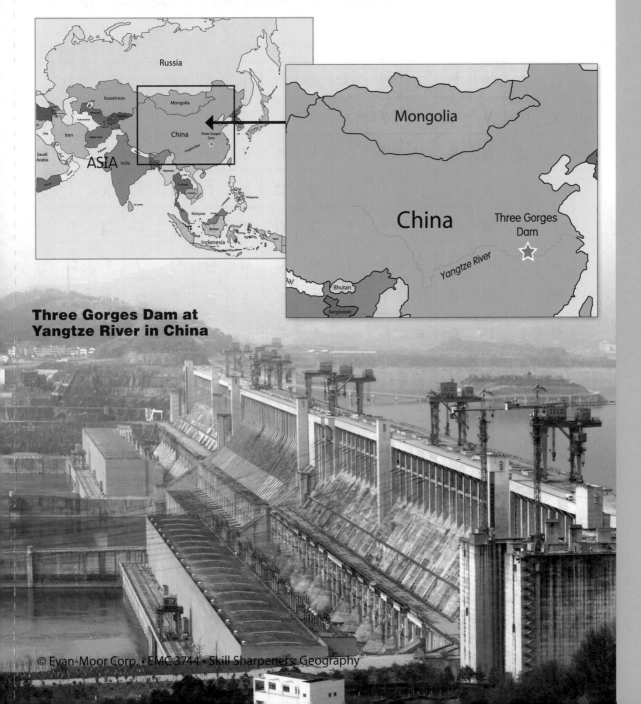

Three Gorges Dam at Yangtze River in China

Environment and Society

Controlling Water

Find these water words in the word search.
Hint: Some are backwards.

pacific	baja	mexico	atlantic
china	panama	isthmus	cape horn
colorado river	three gorges	yangtze	

a	s	r	b	z	d	d	c	h	i	s	w	c	s	z
x	m	y	e	t	z	i	a	p	s	e	z	i	k	q
i	o	a	s	v	t	o	l	e	t	g	l	f	z	j
r	h	x	n	n	i	c	a	p	h	r	a	i	x	f
v	v	w	a	a	r	r	p	d	m	o	j	c	q	o
s	j	l	a	t	p	j	o	c	u	g	g	a	c	a
m	t	s	c	m	r	s	p	d	s	e	r	p	h	t
a	c	a	p	e	h	o	r	n	a	e	u	h	w	l
t	t	o	g	a	y	r	y	l	b	r	j	f	r	a
a	w	u	j	z	c	a	k	z	w	h	o	o	h	n
n	q	a	x	q	n	i	q	f	h	t	i	l	l	t
i	b	c	q	g	j	l	f	s	c	j	t	l	o	i
h	x	c	t	w	c	o	c	i	x	e	m	q	q	c
c	g	z	e	x	j	l	q	s	c	m	t	b	u	v
i	e	n	y	x	q	g	w	u	f	h	x	n	q	i

Skill Sharpeners: Geography • EMC 3744 • © Evan-Moor Corp.

Mapping the Water

Make a map that includes both water and land features.

Skill:
Apply geography concepts in real-world tasks

What You Need

- 11" x 17" (28 x 43 cm) sheet of white construction paper
- pencil
- ruler
- colored pencils

What You Do

1. Create a map of an imaginary landscape that includes the following features:

isthmus	continents	reservoir	strait
long river	dam on the river	two oceans	
locks	ships	hydroelectric plant	

2. Use a pencil to sketch your landscape. Include as many of the features listed above as you can.

3. Once you have finished sketching your map, color it.

4. Label all the features on your map. Then show the map to your family and explain what each feature is.

Environment and Society

Environment and Society

Keep the River Wild?

Make a list of the reasons for and against controlling a river by building a dam. Ask your family for their opinions to add to the list. Then write your final opinion: **Is it best to control a river or keep it wild?**

Pros	Cons
_____	_____
_____	_____
_____	_____
_____	_____
_____	_____

My opinion:

_____

_____

_____

_____

_____

Concept:
Human actions modify the physical environment.

Ask the Astronaut

One of the best days I had at school was when an astronaut came to talk to us. At the end of her presentation, I asked her a question.

"When you are in space, what man-made things are visible on Earth?"

The astronaut smiled. "That is a great question!" she said. "Really, it depends on what your definition of *space* is."

Then she explained. "Most people define *space* as anywhere beyond our atmosphere. What you can see on Earth depends on how far away from our planet you are. But, clearly a few things stand out as man-made. You can see long straight roads in the desert, extended bridges over water, the Great Wall of China, and even some Egyptian pyramids. You can also see city lights at night." Then she added, "We have even spotted large mines in a few areas."

As soon as I got home, I looked up pictures of all the landmarks the astronaut mentioned. They look awesome on Earth, so I can only imagine what they look like from space. Boy, am I glad I asked that question!

Environment and Society

The Great Wall

Define It!

convicts: prisoners

intermittently: every once in a while

angled: placed at an angle to something else

A man-made object that is visible from space is China's Great Wall. It stretches over 13,000 miles (20,921 km).

Construction on the wall began in the 3rd century BC. Sections of the wall were built over time by soldiers, convicts, and common people. Building the wall was a long and difficult task, and many people died during its construction.

The Great Wall of China is made of earth, stone, brick, wood, and other materials. It is 16 feet (4.9 m) tall in some places and 26 feet (7.9 m) tall in others. Guard towers were built intermittently along the wall. The purpose of the Great Wall was to protect China from invasions. Soldiers were stationed along the wall to protect the country.

Astronauts have tried to see how visible the Great Wall is from space. The problem is it blends in well with the landscape. The latest reports are that the Great Wall can be seen only from low orbit space, or just outside the Earth's atmosphere. There also needs to be angled sunlight for it to be visible.

Either way, the Great Wall is one of the most amazing pieces of work ever done on Earth, and it remains a national symbol of China.

Answer the items.

1. Based on the photographs of the Great Wall of China, why do you think constructing the wall was a long and difficult task?

   _____

   _____

2. Would you like to visit the Great Wall of China? Why or why not?

   _____

   _____

Environment and Society

The Great Wall of China

Environment and Society

Concept:
Human actions modify the physical environment.

Open Pit Mines

Define It!

open pit mine: where miners dig out minerals and rocks without making tunnels

excavation: a hole made by digging objects out

orbit: a path in space around the Earth

Open pit mines can be seen from space. An open pit mine is where people dig down and remove rocks or minerals from a pit rather than by tunneling down to get to those objects. One of the world's largest open pit mines is the Bingham Canyon, Kennecott Copper Mine in Utah. It is about 30 miles (48 km) away from Utah's largest city, Salt Lake City. The Kennecott Mine has produced over 18 million tons of copper over its lifetime. Copper is the third most used metal in the world.

The Kennecott Mine is the world's deepest man-made excavation. The mine opened in 1906 and is still in operation today. It is over 2.75 miles (4.4 km) wide and 4,000 feet (1,219 m) deep. Twelve Statue of Liberties stacked on top of each other would not even reach the top of the mine!

Astronauts in orbit can clearly see the Kennecott Mine from space, and they've taken photographs of it. Other mines also visible from space include the Berkeley Pit Mine in Montana, the Escondida Mine in Chile, and the Toquepala Copper Mine in Peru.

Answer the items.

1. Based on the photos, describe an open pit mine.

_____

_____

2. Are you surprised that open pit mines are visible from space? Explain your answer.

_____

_____

Skill Sharpeners: Geography • EMC 3744 • © Evan-Moor Corp.

Kennecott's Bingham Canyon Mine in Utah

Environment and Society

©NASA

Berkeley Pit Mine,
Montana

Toquepala Copper
Mine, Peru

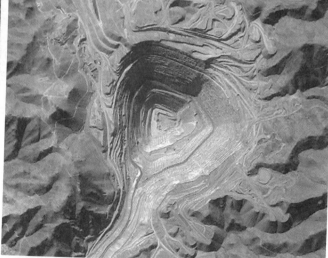

©NASA

Visible from Space

Read the description and write the word it describes.

open pit	copper	invasion
China	convicts	Great Wall
astronaut	excavation	

1. a hole formed by removing earth _____

2. military goes into a country uninvited _____

3. a metallic element in Kennecott Mine _____

4. a person who travels into space _____

5. mining on the surface without tunnels _____

6. prisoners used for work _____

7. 13,000+ miles of protection made of stone, rock, wood, and earth _____

8. country where the Great Wall was built _____

Think About It

Do you think it is possible to hide a large structure on Earth so that it would *not* be visible from space? If so, explain how you would do it. If not, explain why not.

_____

_____

_____

Environment and Society

Where Are They?

On a world map, indicate the structures on Earth that are visible from space.

Skill:
Apply geography concepts in context

What You Need

- Internet access
- world map
- marker or highlighter
- small sticky notes
- pencil or pen

What You Do

1. Print out a map of the world.

2. Look up the man-made landmarks you know can be seen from space as listed in the passages. Find out their locations on Earth.

3. Research to see if there are any other man-made landmarks visible from space that you can add to your list.

4. After you have listed five or more visible landmarks, plot them on the world map.

5. Mark their locations and write the names of the landmarks on sticky notes.

6. Show the map to your family and explain the plots and labels.

Environment and Society

Skill:
Write and draw
to convey
understanding

Hello Down There!

Imagine you are going to design a structure
on Earth that will be visible from space.
What would you include in your design
to make sure space travelers could see it?
Write about it and draw it.

_____

_____

_____

Environment and Society

108

Concept:
The physical environment provides opportunities for human activities.

The AT Trail

My family loves the outdoors, and we have camped and backpacked all my life. Last summer after I turned ten, we decided to hike 100 miles of the Appalachian Trail. We decided to just call it "the AT." We began our journey at the start of the trail at Springer Mountain in Georgia. Then we hiked north, averaging about 10 miles (16 km) a day. The AT Trail goes all the way from where we started to Mount Katahdin in Maine. That's 2,200 miles (3,540 km)! It follows the Appalachian Mountains of the eastern United States.

There were a lot of hikers along the way. Some were just on day hikes. Some, like us, were hiking a section of the AT. Some cruised along at a brisk pace, attempting to hike the whole trail. They walked 20 or more miles (32 km) a day!

There is one thing I remember most about the trail—the shelters along the way. They were three-sided wooden huts. Each hut usually had one or two levels of flat wood for people to put their sleeping bags on and spend the night. We stayed in several of those with lots of other people snoring away after walking miles on the trail that day. We were glad to have the shelters because it kept raining so often.

Next summer when I turn 11, we are going back to the AT to hike 100 more miles!

Environment and Society

PCT

Concept:
The physical environment provides opportunities for human activities.

Environment and Society

There is another long-distance hiking trail on the other side of the United States. It is called the Pacific Crest Trail or PCT. The PCT starts at the United States and Mexico border. From there the trail goes through the southern California desert. Eventually, the PCT climbs into California's Sierra Nevada Mountains. This is the most popular and scenic part of the trail, as it passes through three national parks.

Well into the PCT, it reaches Lassen National Park in Northern California. This is where the Sierra Nevada Mountains end and the Cascade Mountains start. The Cascades are a long series of volcanoes. The PCT then crosses the border into Oregon. It heads through Crater Lake National Park in Oregon and into Washington. The PCT ends in Washington right at the Canadian border.

The whole trail is 2,659 miles (4,279 km) long. A small number of people make the entire journey in 4 to 6 months. They typically start at the south end and hike north so they can get through the desert before summer begins and through the mountains while they are snow-free.

Answer the items.

1. What part of the PCT would you be most interested in seeing? What part would you avoid?

_____

_____

2. What is the longest distance you have hiked? Where was it?

_____

_____

Skill Sharpeners: Geography • EMC 3744 • © Evan-Moor Corp.

Canada
●Manning Park

Washington

▲ Mt. St. Helens

▲ Mt. Hood

Oregon

●Crater Lake

▲ Mt. Shasta

Lassen Volcanic ●
National Park

●South Lake Tahoe

Yosemite
National ●
Park

▲ Mt. Whitney

Kennedy ●
Meadows

●Mojave Desert

California

▲ Mt. Laguna

Campo ●

Mexico

Hikers on a trail in the Cascades, Washington

Crater Lake from the top of Watchman Peak, Oregon

Dirt trail that joins the Pacific Crest Trail in the Mojave Desert wilderness

Environment and Society

Environment and Society

Camino de Santiago

Define It!

annual: yearly or once a year

pilgrimage: a special journey

hostels: places for travelers to stay with shared rooms

St. James the Great was one of Jesus's first disciples. He spread Jesus's message across Spain for almost 40 years. When he died, his remains were taken to Galicia, Spain, where he was buried in a tomb at the Cathedral of Santiago de Compostela. Since then, thousands of people have made an annual pilgrimage to visit his burial site.

There are paths all over Europe to the cathedral. Some paths pass right outside people's homes. The most popular route is known as the "Way of St. James."

Over 250,000 people a year make this trek. Some walk it and others ride a bike. And some go as they did hundreds of years ago, by donkey or horseback. People go for many reasons, including religious or spiritual, reenacting the pilgrimage of long ago.

Along the way, there are hostels with dormitories, or shared rooms, to stay in. They are called "alberques" in Spanish. Trekkers are allowed to stay only one night at each site. The final hostel is called Hostal de los Reyes Catolicos. It is right across from the cathedral where St. James is buried.

Answer the items.

1. Why do you think so many people make this trek?

   _____

   _____

2. Would this be a long-distance hike that would interest you? Why or why not?

   _____

Hostel on the Way
of St. James route
in Logroño, Spain

Route marker along the
Camino de Santiago to the
cathedral – The scallop
shell is the iconic symbol
of the pilgrimage.

Cathedral of
Santiago de
Compostela in
Galicia, Spain

Environment and Society

Long Journey Words

Find these words about long journeys in the word search.
Hint: Some are backwards.

california	canada	cascades
wilderness	hostel	mexico
pilgrimage	scenic	sierra nevada

w	z	i	w	s	h	r	c	l	c	o	s	v	g	w
i	l	b	g	a	n	m	l	h	h	i	v	s	a	s
l	p	i	g	o	u	y	k	y	e	j	f	t	q	h
d	w	n	p	i	a	i	n	r	o	f	i	l	a	c
e	j	f	y	s	b	l	r	s	h	y	f	g	s	b
r	s	o	z	p	c	a	y	e	p	o	a	h	v	c
n	q	q	k	s	n	i	k	d	j	m	s	f	f	o
e	t	s	p	e	s	z	d	a	n	l	x	t	s	w
s	c	a	v	r	k	i	c	c	y	z	u	a	e	j
s	i	a	t	p	c	n	k	s	c	y	d	s	t	l
n	d	t	y	p	h	x	o	a	x	a	y	c	c	o
a	k	k	h	s	z	v	o	c	n	l	s	e	g	t
m	p	i	l	g	r	i	m	a	g	e	g	n	z	g
w	z	z	r	o	i	g	c	l	z	b	b	i	b	w
m	e	x	i	c	o	g	c	j	c	i	w	c	e	q

Your Personal Journey

Find or draw a map of a long journey you have taken.

What You Need

- Internet access
- yellow highlighter
- paper
- colored pencils

What You Do

1. Decide which journey you will map. It could be one you walked, biked, or did on horseback.

2. Use the Internet to find a map of your journey and print it out, or use colored pencils and paper to draw a map.

3. Use the highlighter to trace the route you took on your journey from start to end.

4. Estimate how many miles your journey was and how long it took. Write the details on the map.

5. Write the sights you saw along the way. Sights could include scenery, places you stayed, places you ate, and famous landmarks.

6. Share all the details about your journey with your friends.

Environment and Society

Advertising a Long Journey

What would you say to advertise one of the journeys you read about? What pictures or images would you include? Draw a poster advertising one of the journeys.

Concept:
Places, regions, and environments change over time.

Protecting the Trees

I love protecting nature. Let me take you back over a hundred years ago and tell you about some trees I wish I could have helped save…

It is the 1800s in California's Sierra Nevada Mountains. We are in the presence of the largest trees in the world—sequoias. They are being cut down from a grove called Converse Basin. There are hundreds, maybe thousands, of them being taken away. What is left is a sea of stumps in what was once a huge dense forest.

Sequoias are massive. It can take maybe 20 to 30 people holding hands just to surround the base of one. I guess once you've seen them, you want to save them.

Here in Converse Basin, after being cut, the trees are taken by a plume of water and railroad to mills where they are shaped into lumber for homes, fences, and furniture. It is fascinating watching all the work being done to prepare the trees. There are people cutting them down. Others are slicing logs into smaller sections, making each tree easier to transport. Some trees are transported by train cars onto the flumes, or channels, of water. It is a busy and interesting place for workers…

Back to the present… Sequoias did create a lot of jobs for people. But I guess I wasn't the only one who wanted to save them. Today, sequoias are preserved in groves in three national parks: Sequoia, Kings Canyon, and Yosemite. They are protected in other areas as well.

The Uses of Geography

Seeing Is Believing

Define It!

fossils: ancient remains

circumference: the distance around something

base: the bottom of a tree

Sequoia trees grow naturally only on the western slopes of California's Sierra Nevada Mountains. There are 75 groves left in the wild in that area. There are fossils, or ancient remains, of them growing elsewhere, but not anymore. The climate is perfect for sequoias in the Sierra. The Sierra has cool, wet winters with a lot of snow and mostly dry summers.

Sequoias are larger than any other tree. They are larger than a whale that lives in the ocean, or a dinosaur from the past. They are so massive they have to be seen to be believed. In fact, some people didn't believe the trees were real when they were cut up and shipped to the eastern United States to be put on display. Nonbelievers called them the "California Hoax."

The General Sherman Tree in Sequoia National Park is the world's largest tree. It is over 275 feet (84 m) tall and still growing. And its circumference at the base is over 100 feet (30 m). The General Sherman is also about 2,500 years old. There are some taller trees, but by volume, or because it is so thick, the General Sherman is the most massive tree in the world.

Answer the items.

1. Why do you think people in the eastern United States did not believe sequoia trees were real even after they saw them on display?

_____

_____

2. Do you want to see the sequoia trees? Why or why not?

_____

_____

The General Sherman Tree in Sequoia National Park, California

The Uses of Geography

An Amazing Forest

Define It!

absorb: to soak up

carbon dioxide: pollutant caused by burning coal, oil, and gas

regulate: to control

The Amazon Rainforest is another area with amazing trees. The forested area there makes up more than half of all the world's rainforests.

In the 1960s, people started cutting down parts of the Amazon. They wanted to grow crops on the land. Others wanted to graze cattle there. Many parts of the Amazon were cut down, and some parts were slashed and burned. Movements are now in place to protect the remaining tracts, or areas, of the special forest.

One of the reasons people want to protect the Amazon is that it will help reduce climate change. Trees absorb, or soak up, carbon dioxide. Carbon dioxide is a pollutant made by humans. With higher amounts of it in the Earth's atmosphere, Earth gets warmer. A rainforest such as the Amazon is highly important to help regulate, or control, Earth's temperature by carbon dioxide absorption.

Saving the Amazon is crucial, but cutting parts of it down has allowed some people to make money from crops, cattle, and timber. What will happen to the Amazon in the future is not known, but it is a critical issue.

Answer the item.

What do you think is more important: reducing carbon dioxide or helping people make money from crops, cattle, and timber? Explain your answer.

_____

_____

_____

Skill Sharpeners: Geography • EMC 3744 • © Evan-Moor Corp.

**Slash-and-burn cultivation in the Peruvian Amazon –
This clearing in the rainforest has been planted with
maize seedlings.**

**Deforestation of montane rainforest on the
Amazonian slopes of the Andes in Ecuador –
The forest is being cleared for cattle farming.**

The Uses of Geography

Great Trees and Forests

Solve this crossword puzzle with words about trees and forests.

| grove | circumference | stump | absorb |
| massive | carbon dioxide | base | fossils |

Across

2. bottom part of a tree
4. to soak up
6. distance around something
8. part of cut down tree left in the ground

Down

1. pollutant caused by burning coal, oil, or gas
3. large and heavy
5. group of trees
7. ancient remains

The Uses of Geography

122

How Large Is That Sequoia?

A giant sequoia such as the General Sherman Tree has
a circumference of over 100 feet (30 m) around its base.
Use a tape measure to demonstrate how large around
a giant sequoia is.

What You Need

- several tape measures

- scissors

- large yard space

- string or yarn

What You Do

1. Using the tape measure, measure out 100 feet of string or yarn. You can use more than one tape measure, or use the same tape measure over and over by marking the spot on the string from one measurement to the next until you get to 100 feet.

2. After you have 100 feet of string, lay it out in a circle in a large outdoor space.

3. Invite friends, classmates, and family to see how big the base of a sequoia is. Find out how many people it takes to stand around the circle.

The Uses of Geography

Skill:
Write informative text to convey information and experiences clearly

Saving Trees

If giant sequoias or the Amazon Rainforest are worthy of protection, are other trees as well? Research trees in your area that may need protection. Write to tell about the trees, why they need protection, and what you can do to help save them.

_____

_____

_____

_____

_____

_____

_____

_____

_____

_____

_____

_____

_____

_____

The Uses of Geography

Skill Sharpeners: Geography • EMC 3744 • © Evan-Moor Corp.

Concept:
People can change the geographic characteristics of places, regions, and environments.

Don't Rain on the Olympics!

My family and I love watching the Olympics. We especially enjoy the opening ceremonies and all their glamour. Uncle Ron is a meteorologist. He told me a story about the Beijing, China, Olympics that not very many people know about. It took place at their opening ceremonies in 2008.

Beijing wanted their opening ceremonies to be known as the "biggest party on the planet." But Beijing is also known for its wet, rainy weather. Their main stadium doesn't have a roof. The forecast on the day the world would be watching was as expected—rain.

Before the event, China's government sent 1,100 dispersal rockets into the clouds before they moved over Olympic Stadium. These special rockets carried chemicals in them. The chemicals caused the clouds to release rain away from the opening ceremony. The "weather modification" project was a success, and the event went on as planned without any rain to spoil it.

Uncle Ron called the project a cloud seeding, and he said it is a lot more common than people know.

The Uses of Geography

Making More Rain

Concept:
People can change the geographic characteristics of places, regions, and environments.

The Uses of Geography

Define It!

precipitation: rain, hail, sleet, or snow

silver iodide: a chemical similar to ice crystals

reservoir: a place to store large amounts of water

The world's population keeps growing. People are also moving into areas that don't have enough water. Cloud seeding is a procedure that makes clouds, which are made up of millions of drops of water, release water. This means that more precipitation falls. Precipitation is rain, hail, sleet, or snow. No one knows for sure how much more precipitation cloud seeding produces. But scientists are sure the method works. There just has to be clouds and storms for scientists to seed.

Once storm clouds move over an area, the chemical silver iodide is released in them. It is either dropped from planes into the clouds or released from the ground up. Silver iodide is very similar to ice crystals. Water in the clouds combines with the silver iodide particles, and they become heavy enough to fall out of the cloud as rain.

Cloud seeding is concentrated on areas that benefit from it such as rivers, reservoirs, or lakes where water can be stored for droughts, or long dry seasons. Cloud seeding is used by many countries.

Answer the items.

1. How is the world's population related to cloud seeding?

   _____

   _____

2. Do you think cloud seeding is a good idea? Explain your answer.

   _____

   _____

A cloud combined with silver iodide produces rain.

The Uses of Geography

Stop the Storm!

Define It!

hurricane: the largest storm on Earth

modify: to make partial or minor changes

meteorologist: a weather expert

The Uses of Geography

Hurricanes are the largest and most powerful storms on Earth. They sometimes reach land where large cities are. Scientists have tried to modify, or control, hurricanes to see if they can reduce the storm's impact on people and property. Hurricanes produce damage from incredibly strong winds, heavy rain, and tidal surges of water from the ocean. Project Stormfury was a government attempt to try to reduce the winds of hurricanes by cloud seeding.

Navy jets flew into a storm and released silver iodide. This was coordinated with meteorologists, or weather experts, on the ground who radioed to the pilots when to release the particles. The scientists wanted to make the eyewall of the storm, which is around the very center, weaker. This is where the winds are the strongest.

In the 1960s, four hurricanes were seeded, and it made the hurricanes' winds weaker. But two of the storms regained their intensity. The next day, those storms were just as strong as predicted in the first place.

Hurricane modification ended in 1983. Some say it may come back again once experts have better knowledge and technology to work with.

Answer the item.

Do you think scientists should try cloud seeding hurricanes again? Why or why not?

_____

_____

Skill Sharpeners: Geography • EMC 3744 • © Evan-Moor Corp.

On August 28, 2005, the National Hurricane Center warned that Hurricane Katrina was set to become one of the most powerful storms to strike the United States, with winds of 160 miles (258 km) per hour and stronger gusts.

Two hours after the National Hurricane Center issued their warning, the Moderate Resolution Imaging Spectroradiometer (MODIS) captured this image from NASA's Terra satellite at 1:00 p.m. eastern daylight time. The massive storm covers much of the Gulf of Mexico, spanning from the U.S. coast to the Yucatán Peninsula.

©NASA

The Uses of Geography

Skill:
Apply content
vocabulary

Modifying the Weather

Solve this crossword puzzle about making weather change.

hurricane	modify	cloud seed
silver iodide	meteorologist	beijing
precipitation	rain	

Across

2. to change something
6. largest storm on Earth
7. weather expert
8. chemical added to clouds

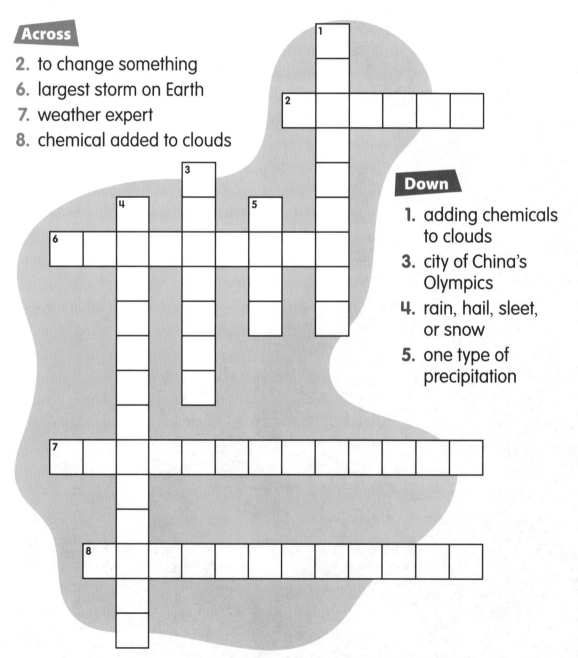

Down

1. adding chemicals to clouds
3. city of China's Olympics
4. rain, hail, sleet, or snow
5. one type of precipitation

The Uses of Geography

130

Make It Rain!

In this activity, you are going to make it rain more than it would have over a small area.

What You Need

- parent supervision
- glass canning jar
- aluminum pie pan
- very hot water
- ice cubes
- flashlight

What You Do

1. Ask an adult to supervise while you do this project.

2. Pour about 2 inches (5 cm) of very hot water into the canning jar.

3. Put 7 or 8 large ice cubes in the pie pan.

4. Place the pie pan on top of the jar.

5. In a darkened room, and while using the flashlight, observe inside the jar and underneath the pie pan for 10 or more minutes. Condensation of water will occur rapidly due to the contrast of temperatures. This will make the underside of the pan start to drip water, or rain. Because of the contrasting, or very different, temperatures in a small area, it will have rained a lot more this way.

The Uses of Geography

Skill:
Write informative text to convey information and experiences clearly

Water Needed!

Cloud seeding is used in about 50 different countries to make more rain. Are there other ways you can think of to produce more water for towns and cities to use in their homes and gardens?

_____

_____

_____

_____

_____

_____

_____

_____

_____

_____

_____

_____

_____

_____

The Uses of Geography

Answer Key

Page 6
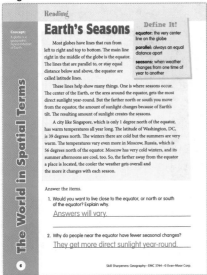

Reading

Earth's Seasons

Define It!
- **equator:** the very center line on the globe
- **parallel:** always an equal distance apart
- **seasons:** when weather changes from one time of year to another

Most globes have lines that run from left to right and top to bottom. The main line right in the middle of the globe is the equator. The lines that are parallel to, or stay equal distance below and above, the equator are called latitude lines.

These lines help show many things. One is where seasons occur. The center of the Earth, or the area around the equator, gets the most direct sunlight year-round. But the farther north or south you move from the equator, the amount of sunlight changes because of Earth's tilt. The resulting amount of sunlight creates the seasons.

A city like Singapore, which is only 1 degree north of the equator, has warm temperatures all year long. The latitude of Washington, DC, is 39 degrees north. The winters there are cold but the summers are very warm. The temperatures vary even more in Moscow, Russia, which is 56 degrees north of the equator. Moscow has very cold winters, and its summer afternoons are cool, too. So, the farther away from the equator a place is located, the cooler the weather gets overall and the more it changes with each season.

Answer the items.

1. Would you want to live close to the equator, or north or south of the equator? Explain why.
   Answers will vary.

2. Why do people near the equator have fewer seasonal changes?
   They get more direct sunlight year-round.

The World in Spatial Terms

Page 8

Reading

East and West

Define It!
- **longitude:** lines that go north to south on a globe
- **prime meridian:** the main line of longitude going through England
- **navigation:** the act of guiding a ship or boat in ocean waters

A globe has lines that go north to south. These are called lines of longitude. One of these lines is called the prime meridian. It goes directly through Greenwich, England. This line is at 0 degrees longitude.

Other longitude lines are shown in degrees east or west of the prime meridian. For example, the city of Auckland, New Zealand, is 174 degrees east longitude. Tokyo, Japan, is 139 degrees east. Beijing, China, is 116 degrees east. Lima, Peru, is 77 degrees west. Mexico City, Mexico, is 99 degrees west. And New York City, New York, in the United States is 74 degrees west longitude.

Knowing longitude and latitude is important for many things, including ocean navigation. Navigation is controlling the movement of a boat or ship from one place to another. Instruments can tell us our ocean location. They can also guide us to desired destinations by using latitude and longitude coordinates.

Answer the items.

1. What is the prime meridian?
   It is the 0 degrees longitude line through England.

2. Can you find your city's nearest longitude line on a globe? What is it, including *east* or *west*?
   Answers will vary.

The World in Spatial Terms

Page 10
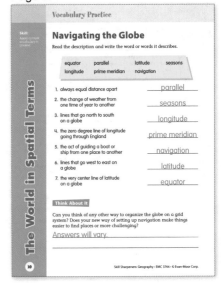

Vocabulary Practice

Navigating the Globe

Read the description and write the word or words it describes.

| equator | parallel | latitude | seasons |
| longitude | prime meridian | navigation | |

1. always equal distance apart — _parallel_
2. the change of weather from one time of year to another — _seasons_
3. lines that go north to south on a globe — _longitude_
4. the zero degree line of longitude going through England — _prime meridian_
5. the act of guiding a boat or ship from one place to another — _navigation_
6. lines that go west to east on a globe — _latitude_
7. the very center line of latitude on a globe — _equator_

Think About It

Can you think of any other way to organize the globe on a grid system? Does your new way of setting up navigation make things easier to find places or more challenging?
Answers will vary.

The World in Spatial Terms

Page 12

Application

Taking Away the Lines

What if there were no such thing as latitude or longitude lines for navigation? How would you describe to someone where something is located on a globe? Try to do it. Describe to someone where something is located on a globe without using latitude and longitude. Write about the challenges you faced and tell if you were able to overcome them.

Writing will vary.

The World in Spatial Terms

Page 14
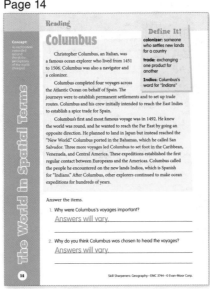

Reading

Columbus

Define It!
- **colonizer:** someone who settles new lands for a country
- **trade:** exchanging one product for another
- **Indios:** Columbus's word for "Indians"

Christopher Columbus, an Italian, was a famous ocean explorer who lived from 1451 to 1506. Columbus was also a navigator and a colonizer.

Columbus completed four voyages across the Atlantic Ocean on behalf of Spain. The journeys to establish permanent settlements and to set up trade routes. Columbus and his crew initially intended to reach the East Indies to establish a spice trade for Spain.

Columbus's first and most famous voyage was in 1492. He knew the world was round, and he wanted to reach the Far East by going an opposite direction. He planned to land in Japan but instead reached the "New World." Columbus ported in the Bahamas, which he called San Salvador. Three more voyages led Columbus to set foot in the Caribbean, Venezuela, and Central America. These expeditions established the first regular contact between Europeans and the Americas. Columbus called the people he encountered on the new lands Indios, which is Spanish for "Indians." After Columbus, other explorers continued to make ocean expeditions for hundreds of years.

Answer the items.

1. Why were Columbus's voyages important?
   Answers will vary.

2. Why do you think Columbus was chosen to head the voyages?
   Answers will vary.

The World in Spatial Terms

Page 16
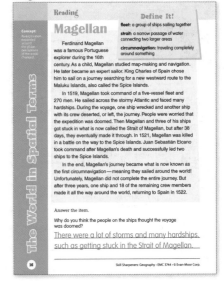

Reading

Magellan

Define It!
- **fleet:** a group of ships sailing together
- **strait:** a narrow passage of water connecting two larger areas
- **circumnavigation:** traveling completely around something

Ferdinand Magellan was a famous Portuguese explorer during the 16th century. As a child, Magellan studied map-making and navigation. He later became an expert sailor. King Charles of Spain chose him to sail on a journey searching for a new westward route to the Maluku Islands, also called the Spice Islands.

In 1519, Magellan took command of a five-vessel fleet and 270 men. He sailed across the stormy Atlantic and faced many hardships. During the voyage, one ship wrecked and another ship with its crew deserted, or left, the journey. People were worried that the expedition was doomed. Then Magellan and three of his ships got stuck in what is now called the Strait of Magellan, but after 38 days, they eventually made it through. In 1521, Magellan was killed in a battle on the way to the Spice Islands. Juan Sebastián Elcano took command after Magellan's death and successfully led two ships to the Spice Islands.

In the end, Magellan's journey became what is now known as the first circumnavigation—meaning they sailed around the world! Unfortunately, Magellan did not complete the entire journey. But after three years, one ship and 18 of the remaining crew members made it all the way around the world, returning to Spain in 1522.

Answer the item.

Why do you think the people on the ships thought the voyage was doomed?
There were a lot of storms and many hardships, such as getting stuck in the Strait of Magellan.

The World in Spatial Terms

Page 18
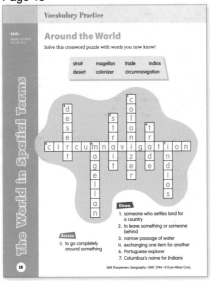

Vocabulary Practice

Around the World

Solve this crossword puzzle with words you now know!

| strait | magellan | trade | indios |
| desert | colonizer | circumnavigation | |

Down
1. someone who settles land for a country
2. to leave something or someone behind
3. narrow passage of water
4. exchanging one item for another
6. Portuguese explorer
7. Columbus's name for Indians

Across
5. to go completely around something

The World in Spatial Terms

Page 20
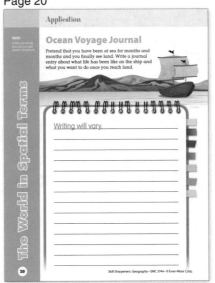

Application

Ocean Voyage Journal

Pretend that you have been at sea for months and months and you finally see land. Write a journal entry about what life has been like on the ship and what you want to do once you reach land.

Writing will vary.

The World in Spatial Terms

Page 22

Reading

New Zealand

Define It!
- **hemisphere:** one half of the Earth
- **glacier:** large sheets of ice that move slowly
- **fiord:** a U-shaped glacier-carved valley that was once flooded by the sea

National parks are special lands that countries preserve and protect. New Zealand, in the Southern Hemisphere, has 13 national parks.

New Zealand is made up of two islands—the North Island and the South Island, which are both long and thin. Starting on the North Island, a popular national park is Tongariro. This national park is New Zealand's oldest, and it has glaciers as well as three active volcanoes.

Most of New Zealand's most famous national parks are on the South Island. Abel Tasman National Park is one known for its incredible beaches. Aoraki/Mount Cook National Park has massive glaciers hanging off its sides. The huge glaciers move slowly downhill. Westland National Park has rainforests and two very large glaciers, the Franz Josef and the Fox.

The country's most famous and its largest national park is Fiordland. It has 14 large fiords that are framed by high mountains, waterfalls, and many lakes and rivers. In 1990, Fiordland was listed as a United Nations World Heritage Site and given the name Te Wahipounamu, meaning "the place of greenstone," after the area's most treasured mineral resource, jade. Fiordland is also where a number of scenes from the movie *Lord of the Rings* were filmed.

Answer the items.

1. Would you like to visit New Zealand's North Island or South Island? Explain your answer.
   Answers will vary.

2. In your opinion, what is the most special thing about Fiordland?
   Answers will vary.

Places and Regions

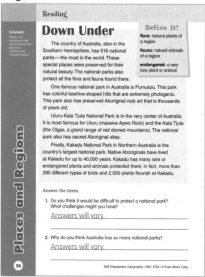

Reading

Concept: Places are locations that have distinctive physical and human characteristics.

Down Under

The country of Australia, also in the Southern Hemisphere, has 516 national parks—the most in the world. These special places were preserved for their natural beauty. The national parks also protect all the flora and fauna found there.

One famous national park in Australia is Purnululu. This park has colorful beehive-shaped hills that are extremely photogenic. This park also has preserved Aboriginal rock art that is thousands of years old.

Uluru-Kata Tjuta National Park is in the very center of Australia. It is most famous for Uluru (massive Ayers Rock) and the Kata Tjuta (the Olgas, a grand range of red domed mountains). The national park also has sacred Aboriginal sites.

Finally, Kakadu National Park in Northern Australia is the country's largest national park. Native Aboriginals have lived at Kakadu for up to 40,000 years. Kakadu has many rare or endangered plants and animals protected there. In fact, more than 280 different types of birds and 2,000 plants flourish at Kakadu.

Define It!
flora: natural plants of a region
fauna: natural animals of a region
endangered: a very rare plant or animal

Answer the items.
1. Do you think it would be difficult to protect a national park? What challenges might you have?
   Answers will vary.
2. Why do you think Australia has so many national parks?
   Answers will vary.

Places and Regions

Vocabulary Practice

Skill: Apply content vocabulary in context

Special Places

Read the description and write the word or words it describes.

| flora | fauna | national park | hemisphere |
| glacier | fiord | endangered | |

1. the animals of a region — **fauna**
2. a special area of land protected by a country — **national park**
3. an ice sheet that slowly melts and moves downhill — **glacier**
4. the plants of a region — **flora**
5. one of two halves of the Earth, divided at the center — **hemisphere**
6. an inland body of water that is deep and narrow and connected to the sea — **fiord**
7. a very rare plant or animal — **endangered**

Think About It

What are some reasons a certain area might be made into a national park? Why would a country want to protect certain lands?
Answers will vary.

Places and Regions

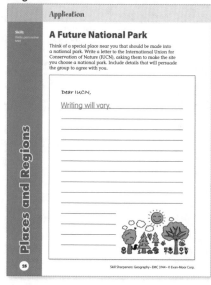

Application

Skill: Write persuasive text

A Future National Park

Think of a special place near you that should be made into a national park. Write a letter to the International Union for Conservation of Nature (IUCN), asking them to make the site you choose a national park. Include details that will persuade the group to agree with you.

Dear IUCN,
Writing will vary.

Places and Regions

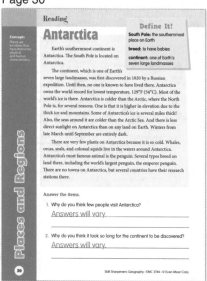

Reading

Concept: Places are locations that have distinctive physical and human characteristics.

Antarctica

Earth's southernmost continent is Antarctica. The South Pole is located on Antarctica.

The continent, which is one of Earth's seven large landmasses, was first discovered in 1820 by a Russian expedition. Until then, no one is known to have lived there. Antarctica owns the world record for lowest temperature, 129°F (54°C). Most of the world's ice is there. Antarctica is colder than the Arctic, where the North Pole is, for several reasons. One is that it is higher in elevation due to the thick ice and mountains. Some of Antarctica's ice is several miles thick! Also, the seas around it are colder than the Arctic Sea. And there is less direct sunlight on Antarctica than on any land on Earth. Winters from late March until September are entirely dark.

There are very few plants on Antarctica because it is so cold. Whales, orcas, seals, and colossal squids live in the waters around Antarctica. Antarctica's most famous animal is the penguin. Several types breed on land there, including the world's largest penguin, the emperor penguin. There are no towns on Antarctica, but several countries have their research stations there.

Define It!
South Pole: the southernmost place on Earth
breed: to have babies
continent: one of Earth's seven large landmasses

Answer the items.
1. Why do you think few people visit Antarctica?
   Answers will vary.
2. Why do you think it took so long for the continent to be discovered?
   Answers will vary.

Places and Regions

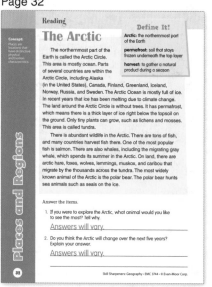

Reading

Concept: Places are locations that have distinctive physical and human characteristics.

The Arctic

The northernmost part of the Earth is called the Arctic Circle. This area is mostly ocean. Parts of several countries are within the Arctic Circle, including Alaska (in the United States), Canada, Finland, Greenland, Iceland, Norway, Russia, and Sweden. The Arctic Ocean is mostly full of ice. In recent years that ice has been melting due to climate change. The land around the Arctic Circle is without trees. It has permafrost, which means there is a thick layer of ice right below the topsoil on the ground. Only tiny plants can grow, such as lichens and mosses. This area is called tundra.

There is abundant wildlife in the Arctic. There are tons of fish, and many countries harvest fish there. One of the most popular fish is salmon. There are also whales, including the migrating gray whale, which spends its summer in the Arctic. On land, there are arctic hare, foxes, wolves, lemmings, muskox, and caribou that migrate by the thousands across the tundra. The most widely known animal of the Arctic is the polar bear. The polar bear hunts sea animals such as seals on the ice.

Define It!
Arctic: the northernmost part of the Earth
permafrost: soil that stays frozen underneath the top layer
harvest: to gather a natural product during a season

Answer the items.
1. If you were to explore the Arctic, what animal would you like to see the most? Tell why.
   Answers will vary.
2. Do you think the Arctic will change over the next five years? Explain your answer.
   Answers will vary.

Places and Regions

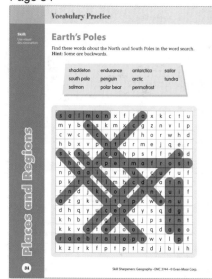

Vocabulary Practice

Skill: Use visual discrimination

Earth's Poles

Find these words about the North and South Poles in the word search.
Hint: Some are backwards.

shackleton	endurance	antarctica	sailor
south pole	penguin	arctic	tundra
salmon	polar bear	permafrost	

Places and Regions

Application

Skill: Write informational text to convey information and experiences clearly

Can You Get Out?

What would you do if your boat was stuck in ice? What special supplies could help you? Remember, the longer you're stuck, the cooler the crew gets and supplies could run out. Write down some of your solutions.

Writing will vary.

Places and Regions

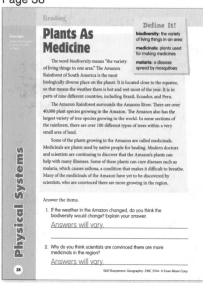

Reading

Concept: Physical processes shape Earth's surface.

Plants As Medicine

The word *biodiversity* means "the variety of living things in one area." The Amazon Rainforest of South America is the most biologically diverse place on the planet. It is located close to the equator, so that means the weather there is hot and wet most of the year. It is in parts of nine different countries, including Brazil, Ecuador, and Peru.

The Amazon Rainforest surrounds the Amazon River. There are over 40,000 plant species growing in the Amazon. The Amazon also has the largest variety of tree species growing in the world. In some sections of the rainforest, there are over 100 different types of trees within a very small area of land.

Some of the plants growing in the Amazon are called medicinals. Medicinals are plants used by native people for healing. Modern doctors and scientists are continuing to discover that the Amazon's plants can help with many illnesses. Some of these plants can cure diseases such as malaria, which causes asthma, a condition that makes it difficult to breathe. Many of the medicinals of the Amazon have yet to be discovered by scientists, who are convinced there are more growing in the region.

Define It!
biodiversity: the variety of living things in an area
medicinals: plants used for making medicines
malaria: a disease spread by mosquitoes

Answer the items.
1. If the weather in the Amazon changed, do you think the biodiversity would change? Explain your answer.
   Answers will vary.
2. Why do you think scientists are convinced there are more medicinals in the region?
   Answers will vary.

Physical Systems

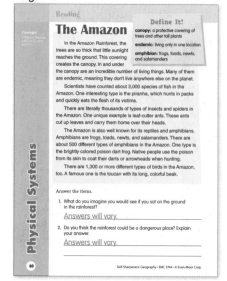

Reading

Concept: Physical processes shape Earth's surface.

The Amazon

In the Amazon Rainforest, the trees are so thick that little sunlight reaches the ground. This covering creates the canopy. In and under the canopy are an incredible number of living things. Many of them are endemic, meaning they don't live anywhere else on the planet.

Scientists have counted about 3,000 species of fish in the Amazon. One interesting type is the piranha, which hunts in packs and quickly eats the flesh of its victims.

There are literally thousands of types of insects and spiders in the Amazon. One unique example is leaf-cutter ants. These ants cut up leaves and carry them home over their heads.

The Amazon is also well known for its reptiles and amphibians. Amphibians are frogs, toads, newts, and salamanders. There are about 500 different types of amphibians in the Amazon. One type is the brightly colored poison dart frog. Native people use the poison from its skin to coat their darts or arrowheads when hunting.

There are 1,300 or more different types of birds in the Amazon, too. A famous one is the toucan with its long, colorful beak.

Define It!
canopy: a protective covering of trees and other tall plants
endemic: living only in one location
amphibian: frogs, toads, newts, and salamanders

Answer the items.
1. What do you imagine you would see if you sat on the ground in the rainforest?
   Answers will vary.
2. Do you think the rainforest could be a dangerous place? Explain your answer.
   Answers will vary.

Physical Systems

Skill Sharpeners: Geography • EMC 3744 • © Evan-Moor Corp.

Page 42

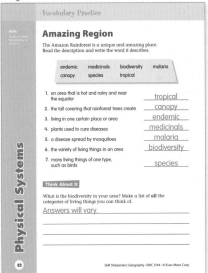

Amazing Region

Vocabulary Practice

The Amazon Rainforest is a unique and amazing place.
Read the description and write the word it describes.

| endemic | medicinals | biodiversity | malaria |
| canopy | species | tropical | |

1. an area that is hot and rainy and near the equator — tropical
2. the tall covering that rainforest trees create — canopy
3. living in one certain place or area — endemic
4. plants used to cure diseases — medicinals
5. a disease spread by mosquitoes — malaria
6. the variety of living things in an area — biodiversity
7. many living things of one type, such as birds — species

Think About It

What is the biodiversity in your area? Make a list of **all** the categories of living things you can think of.
Answers will vary.

Physical Systems

Page 44

Application

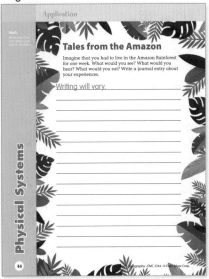

Tales from the Amazon

Imagine that you had to live in the Amazon Rainforest for one week. What would you see? What would you hear? What would you eat? Write a journal entry about your experiences.

Writing will vary.

Physical Systems

Page 46

Reading

Glaciers

Define It!

glacier: a slowly moving field of ice

bergschrund: a large crack near the top of a glacier

moraine: a pile of rocks a glacier pushes ahead of it

glacial erratic: a boulder moved by a glacier and left there

John Muir was fascinated by glaciers. There was so much to know about these huge, slowly moving sheets of ice. One of Muir's favorite places to observe glaciers was in California's Sierra Nevada Mountains, in what is now Yosemite National Park.

Muir went to Yosemite in the late 1800s when there were a few small glaciers in the park. Muir noted the features that made them glaciers. They had a crack, or bergschrund, near the top indicating movement. He also observed crevasses, or cracks within the glacier, showing it was moving downhill. Muir saw moraines, or piles of rock, at the base of the glacier, showing where the ice had pushed the rocks forward.

Muir believed that much larger glaciers had once been there. He observed the deep, U-shaped valleys that were carved by huge glaciers in the Ice Age of the past. The Ice Age was a time when Earth was cooler and there were many glaciers. He also saw shiny, polished rocks. He knew that the rocks became shiny because glaciers had moved over them slowly and smoothed them out. In addition, he saw large boulders in places where they could only be by being moved by a glacier. These boulders are called glacial erratics. People continue to learn more about glaciers every day.

Answer the item.

Can anyone prove that a glacier moves? Explain your answer.
Answers will vary. Example: Yes, if you see a bergschrund at the top and crevasses, it means the glacier is moving.

Physical Systems

Page 48

Reading

Europe's Glaciers

Define It!

Alps: a high mountain range in Europe

latitude: measured distance from the equator

climate change: warmer weather occurring on Earth due, in part, to human activities

Europe has many glaciers. One reason for this is that there are very high mountains in Europe, including the Alps. High mountains lead to colder weather and more snow. Also, much of Europe is far north in latitude, which makes the weather cooler.

Some European countries with glaciers include Switzerland, Austria, Germany, France, and Italy. Europe's largest glacier, though, is in Norway. The Jostedalsbreen Glacier in Norway is 37 miles (60 km) long and 2,000 feet (610 m) thick.

Most of Europe's glaciers are melting because of climate change. In some European locations, countries are trying to slow down glacier melt by covering them with huge white cloths or blankets. White is used because it reflects the sun. The glaciers are also being covered to help prevent ski resorts from losing business due to shorter seasons. Also, towns below the glacier depend on the glacial ice melting slowly as a consistent water source. Slowing down the melt of the glacier ensures that these towns will have the glacier's water longer.

Answer the item.

What else do you think could be done to protect the glaciers in Europe?
Answers will vary.

Physical Systems

Page 50

Vocabulary Practice

Glacier Words

Find these glacier words in the word search.
Hint: Some are backwards.

| moraine | bergschrund | alps | latitude |
| glacier | climate change | muir | |

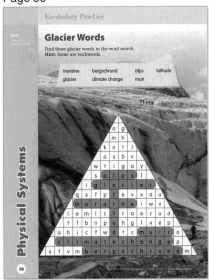

Physical Systems

Page 52

Application

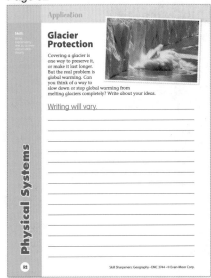

Glacier Protection

Covering a glacier is one way to preserve it, or make it last longer. But the real problem is global warming. Can you think of a way to slow down or stop global warming from melting glaciers completely? Write about your ideas.

Writing will vary.

Physical Systems

Page 54

Reading

Temperate Rainforests

Define It!

conifers: trees that stay green all year

deciduous: trees that lose their leaves in fall

epiphyte: a plant that grows harmlessly on another plant

The Olympic Rainforest in Washington is a temperate rainforest. This means the forest has warm, mostly dry summers, but long, cool, and wet winters. Temperate rainforests are mostly located in what is called the "Roaring 40s" latitude zone. This part of the Earth gets strong winds that drive storms toward land. Also, the inland mountains block the storms, making them drop extra rain on the forest. The trees are a mix of conifers and deciduous. Some plants are epiphytes—they grow right off other plants. Some fallen trees become nurse logs, meaning other plants and trees sprout right on the logs and grow from them. Temperate rainforests occur in only a few parts of the Earth. Some well-known temperate rainforests are on the west coast of the United States from Northern California to Alaska. They are also in western New Zealand's South Island and in Tasmania of Australia. Norway, Peru, and Argentina also have small strips of temperate rainforests.

Answer the items.

1. How would you describe a temperate rainforest?
Answers will vary.

2. What part of the temperate rainforest interests you the most?
Answers will vary.

Physical Systems

Page 56

Reading

Gondwana

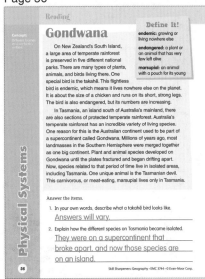

Define It!

endemic: growing or living nowhere else

endangered: a plant or an animal that has very few left alive

marsupial: an animal with a pouch for its young

On New Zealand's South Island, a large area of temperate rainforest is preserved in five different national parks. There are many types of plants, animals, and birds living there. One special bird is the takahē. This flightless bird is endemic, which means it lives nowhere else on the planet. It is about the size of a chicken and runs on its short, strong legs. The bird is also endangered, but its numbers are increasing.

In Tasmania, an island south of Australia's mainland, there are also sections of protected temperate rainforest. Australia's temperate rainforest has an incredible variety of living species. One reason for this is the Australian continent used to be part of a supercontinent called Gondwana. Millions of years ago, most landmasses in the Southern Hemisphere were merged together as one big continent. Plant and animal species developed on Gondwana until the plates fractured and began drifting apart. Now, species related to that period of time live in isolated areas, including Tasmania. One unique animal is the Tasmanian devil. This carnivorous, or meat-eating, marsupial lives only in Tasmania.

Answer the items.

1. In your own words, describe what a takahē bird looks like.
Answers will vary.

2. Explain how the different species on Tasmania became isolated.
They were on a supercontinent that broke apart, and now those species are on an island.

Physical Systems

Page 58

Vocabulary Practice

Special Rainforests

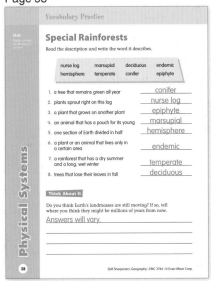

Read the description and write the word it describes.

| nurse log | marsupial | deciduous | endemic |
| hemisphere | temperate | conifer | epiphyte |

1. a tree that remains green all year — conifer
2. plants sprout right on this log — nurse log
3. a plant that grows on another plant — epiphyte
4. an animal that has a pouch for its young — marsupial
5. one section of Earth divided in half — hemisphere
6. a plant or an animal that lives only in a certain area — endemic
7. a rainforest that has a dry summer and a long, wet winter — temperate
8. trees that lose their leaves in fall — deciduous

Think About It

Do you think Earth's landmasses are still moving? If so, tell where you think they might be millions of years from now.
Answers will vary.

Physical Systems

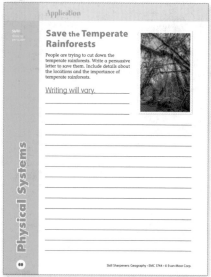

Application

Save the Temperate Rainforests

People are trying to cut down the temperate rainforests. Write a persuasive letter to save them. Include details about the locations and the importance of temperate rainforests.

Writing will vary.

Physical Systems

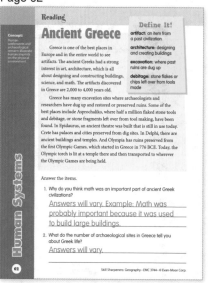

Reading

Ancient Greece

Define It!

artifact: an item from a past civilization

architecture: designing and creating buildings

excavation: where past ruins are dug up

debitage: stone flakes or chips left over from tools made

Greece is one of the best places in Europe and in the entire world to see artifacts. The ancient Greeks had a strong interest in art, architecture, which is all about designing and constructing buildings, science, and math. The artifacts discovered in Greece are 2,000 to 4,000 years old.

Greece has many excavation sites where archaeologists and researchers have dug up and restored or preserved ruins. Some of the best places include Asprochaliko, where half a million flaked stone tools and debitage, or stone fragments left over from tool making, have been found. In Epidaurus, an ancient theatre was built that is still in use today. Crete has palaces and cities preserved from dig sites. In Delphi, there are ancient buildings and temples. And Olympia has ruins preserved from the first Olympic Games, which started in Greece in 776 BCE. Today, the Olympic torch is lit at a temple there and then transported to wherever the Olympic Games are being held.

Answer the items.

1. Why do you think math was an important part of ancient Greek civilizations?
   Answers will vary. Example: Math was probably important because it was used to build large buildings.

2. What do the number of archaeological sites in Greece tell you about Greek life?
   Answers will vary.

Human Systems

Reading

How Old Is It?

Define It!

archaeologist: someone who studies ancient civilizations

carbon: an element in all living things

decay: to break down or fall apart over time

Archaeologists find artifacts all over the world. In doing so, they learn about how people lived and what their beliefs may have been.

Archaeologists often make surprising discoveries. For example, 100,000-year-old shells used as jewelry were discovered at Skhul Cave in Israel. At Sibudu Cave in South Africa, archaeologists found tools that were 77,000 years old. The world's oldest bow, as used for hunting with a bow and arrow, was found in Denmark. It is estimated to be 8,000 years old.

There are several ways archaeologists date how old an item is. One is to carefully examine the rock layer the artifact was found in. Scientists can determine how old the soil is and relate the soil's age to the item. Archaeologists can also compare artifacts to each other to determine how old they are. Another way to determine the age of an item is radiocarbon dating. Carbon is an element in all living things. As living things die and decay, they release carbon. The carbon they release is at a constant rate and at set amounts. So scientists can measure how much carbon is left in an item and determine how old the artifact is.

Answer the items.

1. Which method would you use to determine how old an artifact is? Explain why.
   Answers will vary.

2. Do you think there are more artifacts to be discovered? Why haven't people found all of them yet?
   Answers will vary.

Human Systems

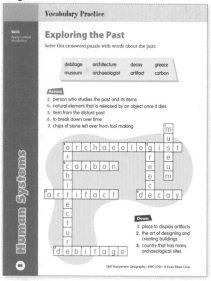

Vocabulary Practice

Exploring the Past

Solve this crossword puzzle with words about the past.

| debitage | architecture | decay | greece |
| museum | archaeologist | artifact | carbon |

Across
2. person who studies the past and its items
4. natural element that is released by an object once it dies
5. item from the distant past
6. to break down over time
7. chips of stone left over from tool making

Down
1. place to display artifacts
2. the art of designing and creating buildings
3. country that has many archaeological sites

(crossword answers: archaeologist, carbon, artifact, decay, debitage, museum)

Human Systems

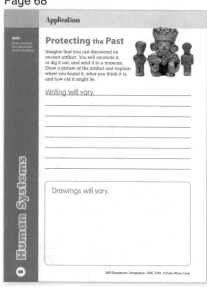

Application

Protecting the Past

Imagine that you just discovered an ancient artifact. You will excavate it, or dig it out, and send it to a museum. Draw a picture of the artifact and explain where you found it, what you think it is, and how old it might be.

Writing will vary.

Drawings will vary.

Human Systems

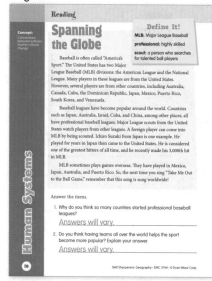

Reading

Spanning the Globe

Define It!

MLB: Major League Baseball

professional: highly skilled

scout: a person who searches for talented ball players

Baseball is often called "America's Sport." The United States has two Major League Baseball (MLB) divisions: the American League and the National League. Many players in these leagues are from the United States. However, several players are from other countries, including Australia, Canada, Cuba, the Dominican Republic, Japan, Mexico, Puerto Rico, South Korea, and Venezuela.

Baseball leagues have become popular around the world. Countries such as Japan, Australia, Israel, Cuba, and China, among other places, all have professional baseball leagues. Major League scouts from the United States watch players from other leagues. A foreign player can come into MLB by being scouted. Ichiro Suzuki from Japan is one example. He played for years in Japan then came to the United States. He is considered one of the greatest hitters of all time, and he recently made his 3,000th hit in MLB.

MLB sometimes plays games overseas. They have played in Mexico, Japan, Australia, and Puerto Rico. So, the next time you sing "Take Me Out to the Ball Game," remember that this song is sung worldwide!

Answer the items.

1. Why do you think so many countries started professional baseball leagues?
   Answers will vary.

2. Do you think having teams all over the world helps the sport become more popular? Explain your answer.
   Answers will vary.

Human Systems

Reading

Negro Leagues

Define It!

Negro League: a baseball league formed by African Americans

recruited: enlisted a person to work for you

Professional baseball leagues have existed since the late 1800s. Because of discrimination, African American players were not welcome to play on Major League Baseball teams. In 1920, African Americans formed the Negro National League. They played in the United States, Canada, and sometimes Latin America.

In 1945, Jackie Robinson was recruited from the Kansas City Monarchs, a Negro League team, into Major League Baseball. Robinson joined the Brooklyn Dodgers in 1947, becoming the first African American to play in MLB.

In 1960, the Negro Leagues came to an end as many of their best players were recruited into the Major Leagues. While this was a great opportunity for the players, it was not without its challenges and struggles. Two of the Negro Leagues' most famous players were:

Satchel Paige: He was a pitcher for the Monarchs from 1926 until 1947. At 42 years old, he made it into the Major Leagues and played for 6 years. He also played one year at age 59!

Josh Gibson: He played in the Negro Leagues for 16 years and hit 800 home runs! He was a catcher, and he is thought of as the best hitter of all time in the Negro Leagues.

Answer the item.

Do you think a person's ethnicity should matter when it comes to playing a sport? Explain your answer.
Answers will vary.

Human Systems

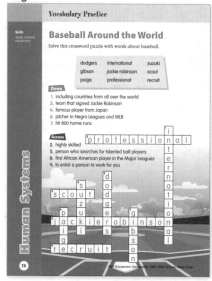

Vocabulary Practice

Baseball Around the World

Solve this crossword puzzle with words about baseball.

dodgers	international	suzuki
gibson	jackie robinson	scout
paige	professional	recruit

Down
1. including countries from all over the world
3. team that signed Jackie Robinson
4. famous player from Japan
6. pitcher in Negro Leagues and MLB
7. hit 800 home runs

Across
2. highly skilled
5. person who searches for talented ball players
8. first African American player in the Major Leagues
9. to enlist a person to work for you

(crossword answers: professional, international, dodgers, scout, suzuki, paige, gibson, jackie robinson, recruit)

Human Systems

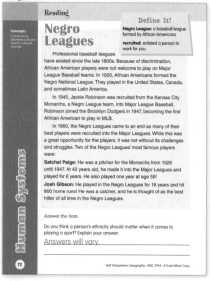

Application

Baseball Connections

Can people learn about different cultures by watching or playing a sport? Do you think the game of baseball helps connect people from around the world? Write your opinions to answer these questions.

Writing will vary.

Human Systems

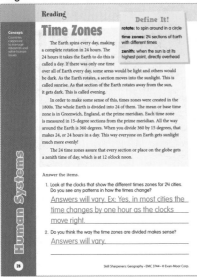

Reading

Time Zones

Define It!

rotate: to spin around in a circle

time zones: 24 sections of Earth with different times

zenith: when the sun is at its highest point, directly overhead

The Earth spins every day, making a complete rotation in 24 hours. The 24 hours it takes the Earth to do this is called a day. If there was only one time over all of Earth every day, some areas would be light and others would be dark. As the Earth rotates, a section moves into the sunlight. This is called sunrise. As that section of the Earth rotates away from the sun, it gets dark. This is called evening.

In order to make some sense of this, times zones were created in the 1800s. The whole Earth is divided into 24 of them. The mean or base time zone is in Greenwich, England, at the prime meridian. Each time zone is measured in 15-degree sections from the prime meridian. All the way around the Earth is 360 degrees. When you divide 360 by 15 degrees, that makes 24, or 24 hours in a day. This way everyone on Earth gets sunlight much more evenly!

The 24 time zones assure that every section or place on the globe gets a zenith time of day, which is at 12 o'clock noon.

Answer the items.

1. Look at the clocks that show the different times zones for 24 cities. Do you see any patterns in how the times change?

<u>Answers will vary. Ex: Yes, in most cities the</u>
<u>time changes by one hour as the clocks</u>
<u>move right.</u>

2. Do you think the way the time zones are divided makes sense?

<u>Answers will vary.</u>

Human Systems

78

Skill Sharpeners: Geography • EMC 3744 • © Evan-Moor Corp.

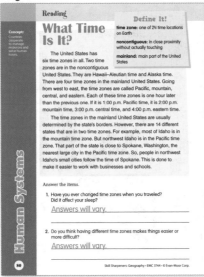

Reading

What Time Is It?

Define It!

time zone: one of 24 time locations on Earth

noncontiguous: in close proximity without actually touching

mainland: main part of the United States

The United States has six time zones in all. Two time zones are in the noncontiguous United States. They are Hawaii–Aleutian time and Alaska time. There are four time zones in the mainland United States. Going from west to east, the time zones are called Pacific, mountain, central, and eastern. Each of these time zones is one hour later than the previous one. If it is 1:00 p.m. Pacific time, it is 2:00 p.m. mountain time, 3:00 p.m. central time, and 4:00 p.m. eastern time.

The time zones in the mainland United States are usually determined by the state's borders. However, there are 14 different states that are in two time zones. For example, most of Idaho is in the mountain time zone. But northwest Idaho is in the Pacific time zone. That part of the state is close to Spokane, Washington, the nearest large city in the Pacific time zone. So, people in northwest Idaho's small cities follow the time of Spokane. This is done to make it easier to work with businesses and schools.

Answer the items.

1. Have you ever changed time zones when you traveled? Did it affect your sleep?

<u>Answers will vary.</u>

2. Do you think having different time zones makes things easier or more difficult?

<u>Answers will vary.</u>

Human Systems

80

Skill Sharpeners: Geography • EMC 3744 • © Evan-Moor Corp.

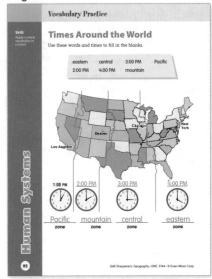

Vocabulary Practice

Times Around the World

Use these words and times to fill in the blanks.

| eastern | central | 3:00 PM | Pacific |
| 2:00 PM | 4:00 PM | mountain | |

1:00 PM — Pacific zone
2:00 PM — mountain zone
3:00 PM — central zone
4:00 PM — eastern zone

Human Systems

82

Skill Sharpeners: Geography • EMC 3744 • © Evan-Moor Corp.

Application

Oh, the Places I Will Go!

Pretend that you are traveling around the globe. Write several journal entries to tell where you have been, what the time difference is, and how you are coping with jet lag.

Date: _____
<u>Writing will vary.</u>

Date: _____

Date: _____

Human Systems

84

Skill Sharpeners: Geography • EMC 3744 • © Evan-Moor Corp.

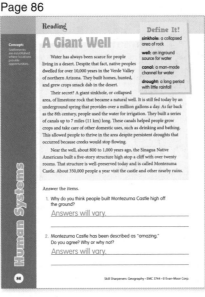

Reading

A Giant Well

Define It!

sinkhole: a collapsed area of rock

well: an inground source for water

canal: a man-made channel for water

drought: a long period with little rainfall

Water has always been scarce for people living in a desert. Despite that fact, native peoples dwelled for over 10,000 years in the Verde Valley of northern Arizona. They built homes, hunted, and grew crops smack dab in the desert.

Their secret? A giant sinkhole, or collapsed area, of limestone rock that became a natural well. It is still fed today by an underground spring that provides over a million gallons a day. As far back as the 8th century, people used the water for irrigation. They built a series of canals up to 7 miles (11 km) long. These canals helped people grow crops and take care of other domestic uses, such as drinking and bathing. This allowed people to thrive in the area despite persistent droughts that occurred because creeks would stop flowing.

Near the well, about 800 to 1,000 years ago, the Sinagua Native Americans built a five-story structure high atop a cliff with over twenty rooms. That structure is well-preserved today and is called Montezuma Castle. About 350,000 people a year visit the castle and other nearby ruins.

Answer the items.

1. Why do you think people built Montezuma Castle high off the ground?

<u>Answers will vary.</u>

2. Montezuma Castle has been described as "amazing." Do you agree? Why or why not?

<u>Answers will vary.</u>

Human Systems

86

Skill Sharpeners: Geography • EMC 3744 • © Evan-Moor Corp.

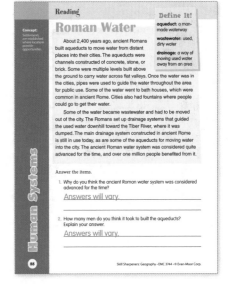

Reading

Roman Water

Define It!

aqueduct: a man-made waterway

wastewater: used, dirty water

drainage: a way of moving used water away from an area

About 2,400 years ago, ancient Romans built aqueducts to move water from distant places into their cities. The aqueducts were channels constructed of concrete, stone, or brick. Some were multiple levels built above the ground to carry water across flat valleys. Once the water was in the cities, pipes were used to guide the water throughout the area for public use. Some of the water went to bath houses, which were common in ancient Rome. Cities also had fountains where people could go to get their water.

Some of the water became wastewater and had to be moved out of the city. The Romans set up drainage systems that guided the used water downhill toward the Tiber River, where it was dumped. The main drainage system constructed in ancient Rome is still in use today, as are some of the aqueducts for moving water into the city. The ancient Roman water system was considered quite advanced for the time, and over one million people benefited from it.

Answer the items.

1. Why do you think the ancient Roman water system was considered advanced for the time?

<u>Answers will vary.</u>

2. How many men do you think it took to built the aqueducts? Explain your answer.

<u>Answers will vary.</u>

Human Systems

88

Skill Sharpeners: Geography • EMC 3744 • © Evan-Moor Corp.

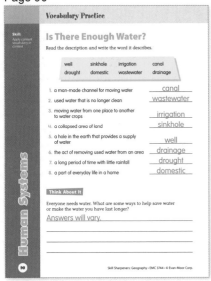

Vocabulary Practice

Is There Enough Water?

Read the description and write the word it describes.

| well | sinkhole | irrigation | canal |
| drought | domestic | wastewater | drainage |

1. a man-made channel for moving water — <u>canal</u>
2. used water that is no longer clean — <u>wastewater</u>
3. moving water from one place to another to water crops — <u>irrigation</u>
4. a collapsed area of land — <u>sinkhole</u>
5. a hole in the earth that provides a supply of water — <u>well</u>
6. the act of removing used water from an area — <u>drainage</u>
7. a long period of time with little rainfall — <u>drought</u>
8. a part of everyday life in a home — <u>domestic</u>

Think About It

Everyone needs water. What are some ways to help save water or make the water you have last longer?

<u>Answers will vary.</u>

Human Systems

90

Skill Sharpeners: Geography • EMC 3744 • © Evan-Moor Corp.

Application

Changing the Land

The ancient Romans built aqueducts. The Sinagua peoples built Montezuma Castle. How did their actions change the land? Do you think they made positive changes? Write about it.

<u>Writing will vary.</u>

Human Systems

92

Skill Sharpeners: Geography • EMC 3744 • © Evan-Moor Corp.

Reading

Panama Canal

Define It!

isthmus: a thin strip of land connecting two seas or oceans

strait: a narrow passage of water connecting two seas

freighter: a ship carrying products

Another area of controlled water is the Panama Canal. Panama is a small, narrow country in Central America. It connects North and South America. Since the age of great ocean explorers in the 1500s, there was talk about connecting the Atlantic and Pacific Oceans through the Isthmus of Panama. An isthmus is a thin strip of land with a large sea or ocean on either side. Ships had to go all the way around South America, passing through the Strait of Magellan. It was a long and difficult journey, taking 3 to 6 months. The Strait of Magellan is known for its treacherous high waves, storms, and strong winds.

France began work on the Panama Canal in 1881. But work on the project was stopped in 1889 due to torrential rains, landslides, and tropical diseases carried by mosquitoes.

The United States took over in 1904. They used the military to help out, as well as mosquito-control techniques. When the U.S. finished the canal in 1914, it was the most expensive project they had ever completed.

Tens of thousands of freighters, or ships carrying goods, now travel through the canal, saving months of ocean journey. Ocean travel from the Atlantic Ocean to the Pacific Ocean can now be completed in 6 to 8 hours.

Answer the items.

1. Why was the Panama Canal built?

<u>It makes travel between the Atlantic and</u>
<u>Pacific Oceans faster and easier.</u>

2. What did the United States do to successfully complete the canal?

<u>They brought in the military and controlled</u>
<u>the mosquitoes.</u>

Environment and Society

94

Skill Sharpeners: Geography • EMC 3744 • © Evan-Moor Corp.

Page 96

Reading

Three Gorges Dam

Concept: People use technology to get what they need from the physical environment.

hydroelectric: using moving water to produce electricity

turbine: an engine with spinning blades inside it

green energy: power without using fossil fuels

The Three Gorges Dam and power station in China is the world's largest hydroelectric dam. *Hydroelectric* means that it takes water and moves it through turbines to create electricity. A turbine is a mechanical device with blades that spin, which helps make the electricity.

The Three Gorges Dam has a huge reservoir, or area of water, behind it. This allows large ships called freighters to sail into inland China rather than just dock at ports. The dam also controls flooding that often occurs on the Yangtze River.

Over one million people were forced to move from their homes, towns, and cities before the dam was built. These areas are now flooded under water. The river's course was changed due to the dam, and this altered fishing as well as other habitats. The water flow was also changed, which causes landslides downstream.

Still, the dam and power station have given China a huge source of green energy. Green means they don't have to burn as much fossil fuels to make power. Fossil fuels are coal, oil, and gas.

Answer the items.

1. What are some benefits of the Three Gorges Dam?
   Large ships can sail into inland China, floods are prevented, and China has some green energy.

2. What are some problems the dam has caused?
   People had to move, fishing was affected, and landslides occur.

Skill Sharpeners: Geography • EMC 3744 • © Evan-Moor Corp.

Page 98

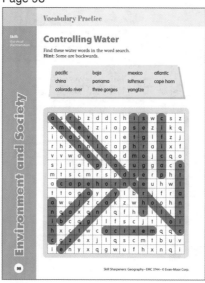

Vocabulary Practice

Controlling Water

Skill: Use the visual discrimination

Find these water words in the word search.
Hint: Some are backwards.

pacific	baja	mexico	atlantic
china	panama	isthmus	cape horn
colorado river	three gorges	yangtze	

Skill Sharpeners: Geography • EMC 3744 • © Evan-Moor Corp.

Page 100

Application

Keep the River Wild?

Skill: Write informative/explanatory information and experiences clearly

Make a list of the reasons for and against controlling a river by building a dam. Ask your family for their opinions to add to the list. Then write your final opinion: Is it best to control a river or keep it wild?

Pros	Cons
Writing will vary.	

My opinion:

Skill Sharpeners: Geography • EMC 3744 • © Evan-Moor Corp.

Page 102

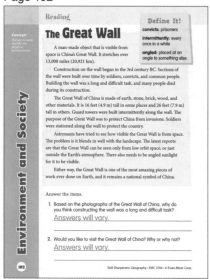

Reading

The Great Wall

Concept: Human beings modify the physical environment.

convicts: prisoners

intermittently: every once in a while

angled: placed at an angle to something else

A man-made object that is visible from space is China's Great Wall. It stretches over 13,000 miles (20,921 km).

Construction on the wall began in the 3rd century BC. Sections of the wall were built over time by soldiers, convicts, and common people. Building the wall was a long and difficult task, and many people died during its construction.

The Great Wall of China is made of earth, stone, brick, wood, and other materials. It is 16 feet (4.9 m) tall in some places and 26 feet (7.9 m) tall in others. Guard towers were built intermittently along the wall. The purpose of the Great Wall was to protect China from invasions. Soldiers were stationed along the wall to protect the country.

Astronauts have tried to see how visible the Great Wall is from space. The problem is it blends in well with the landscape. The latest reports are that the Great Wall can be seen only from low orbit space, or just outside the Earth's atmosphere. There also needs to be angled sunlight for it to be visible.

Either way, the Great Wall is one of the most amazing pieces of work ever done on Earth, and it remains a national symbol of China.

Answer the items.

1. Based on the photographs of the Great Wall of China, why do you think constructing the wall was a long and difficult task?
   Answers will vary.

2. Would you like to visit the Great Wall of China? Why or why not?
   Answers will vary.

Skill Sharpeners: Geography • EMC 3744 • © Evan-Moor Corp.

Page 104

Reading

Open Pit Mines

Concept: Human actions modify the physical environment.

open pit mine: where miners dig out minerals and rocks without making tunnels

excavation: a hole made by digging

orbit: a path in space around the Earth

Open pit mines can be seen from space. An open pit mine is where people dig down and remove rocks or minerals from a pit rather than by tunneling down to get to those objects. One of the world's largest open pit mines is the Bingham Canyon, Kennecott Copper Mine in Utah. It is about 30 miles (48 km) away from Utah's largest city, Salt Lake City. The Kennecott Mine has produced over 18 million tons of copper over its lifetime. Copper is the third most used metal in the world.

The Kennecott Mine is the world's deepest man-made excavation. The mine opened in 1906 and is still in operation today. It is over 2.75 miles (4.4 km) wide and 4,000 feet (1,219 m) deep. Twelve Statue of Liberties stacked on top of each other would not even reach the top of the mine!

Astronauts in orbit can clearly see the Kennecott Mine from space, and they've taken photographs of it. Other mines also visible from space include the Berkeley Pit Mine in Montana, the Escondida Mine in Chile, and the Toquepala Copper Mine in Peru.

Answer the items.

1. Based on the photos, describe an open pit mine.
   Answers will vary.

2. Are you surprised that open pit mines are visible from space? Explain your answer.
   Answers will vary.

Skill Sharpeners: Geography • EMC 3744 • © Evan-Moor Corp.

Page 106

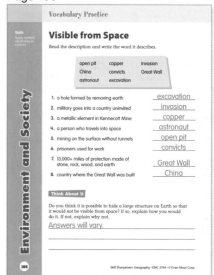

Vocabulary Practice

Visible from Space

Skill: Apply content-area vocabulary in context

Read the description and write the word it describes.

open pit	copper	invasion
China	convicts	Great Wall
astronaut	excavation	

1. a hole formed by removing earth — excavation
2. military goes into a country uninvited — invasion
3. a metallic element in Kennecott Mine — copper
4. a person who travels into space — astronaut
5. mining on the surface without tunnels — open pit
6. prisoners used for work — convicts
7. 13,000+ miles of protection made of stone, rock, wood, and earth — Great Wall
8. country where the Great Wall was built — China

Think About It

Do you think it is possible to hide a large structure on Earth so that it would *not* be visible from space? If so, explain how you would do it. If not, explain why not.
Answers will vary.

Skill Sharpeners: Geography • EMC 3744 • © Evan-Moor Corp.

Page 108

Application

Hello Down There!

Skill: Write and draw to show understanding

Imagine you are going to design a structure on Earth that will be visible from space. What would you include in your design to make sure space travelers could see it? Write about it and draw it.

Writing will vary.

Drawings will vary.

Skill Sharpeners: Geography • EMC 3744 • © Evan-Moor Corp.

Page 110

Reading

PCT

Concept: The physical environment provides opportunities for human activities.

scenic: a view of natural beauty

wilderness: a wild and natural area with few people

Cascades: a mountain range that is volcanic

There is another long-distance hiking trail on the other side of the United States. It is called the Pacific Crest Trail or PCT. The PCT starts at the United States and Mexico border. From there the trail goes through the southern California desert. Eventually, the PCT climbs into California's Sierra Nevada Mountains. This is the most popular and scenic part of the trail, as it passes through three national parks.

Well into the PCT, it reaches Lassen National Park in Northern California. This is where the Sierra Nevada Mountains end and the Cascade Mountains start. The Cascades are a long series of volcanoes. The PCT then crosses the border into Oregon. It heads through Crater Lake National Park in Oregon and into Washington. The PCT ends in Washington right at the Canadian border.

The whole trail is 2,659 miles (4,279 km) long. A small number of people make the entire journey in 4 to 6 months. They typically start at the south end and hike north so they can get through the desert before summer begins and through the mountains while they are snow-free.

Answer the items.

1. What part of the PCT would you be most interested in seeing? What part would you avoid?
   Answers will vary.

2. What is the longest distance you have hiked? Where was it?
   Answers will vary.

Skill Sharpeners: Geography • EMC 3744 • © Evan-Moor Corp.

Page 112

Reading

Camino de Santiago

Concept: The physical environment provides opportunities for human activities.

annual: yearly or once a year

pilgrimage: a special journey

hostels: places for travelers to stay with shared rooms

St. James the Great was one of Jesus's first disciples. He spread Jesus's message across Spain for almost 40 years. When he died, his remains were taken to Galicia, Spain, where he was buried in a tomb at the Cathedral of Santiago de Compostela. Since then, thousands of people have made an annual pilgrimage to visit his burial site.

There are paths all over Europe to the cathedral. Some paths pass right outside people's homes. The most popular route is known as the "Way of St. James."

Over 250,000 people a year make this trek. Some walk it and others ride a bike. And some go as they did hundreds of years ago, by donkey or horseback. People go for many reasons, including religious or spiritual, reenacting the pilgrimage of long ago.

Along the way, there are hostels with dormitories, or shared rooms, to stay in. They are called "albergues" in Spanish. Trekkers are allowed to stay only one night at each site. The final hostel is called Hostal de los Reyes Catolicos. It is right across from the cathedral where St. James is buried.

Answer the items.

1. Why do you think so many people make this trek?
   Answers will vary.

2. Would this be a long-distance hike that would interest you? Why or why not?
   Answers will vary.

Skill Sharpeners: Geography • EMC 3744 • © Evan-Moor Corp.

Skill Sharpeners: Geography • EMC 3744 • © Evan-Moor Corp.

Page 114

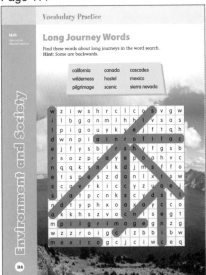

Page 116

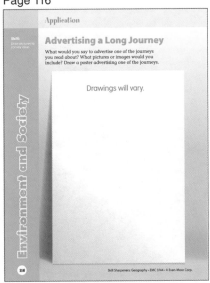

Page 118

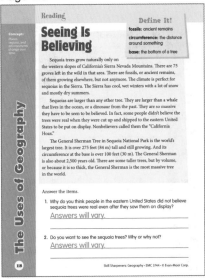

Page 120

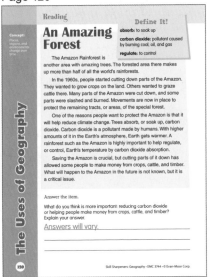

Page 122

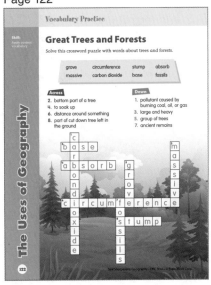

Page 124

Page 126

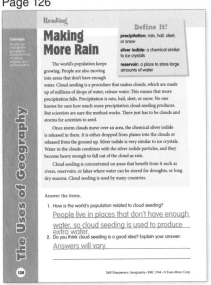

Page 128

Page 130

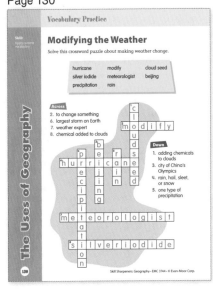

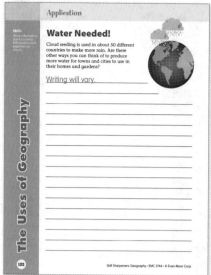

Application

Water Needed!

Cloud seeding is used in about 50 different countries to make more rain. Are there other ways you can think of to produce more water for towns and cities to use in their homes and gardens?

Writing will vary.

_____

_____

_____

_____

_____

_____

_____

_____

_____

_____

_____

_____

_____

_____

The Uses of Geography

132

Notes